Standard English Program
Consolidated Programs Department
West Contra Costa USD

SPEAK STANDARD, TOO

Add Mainstream American English To Your Talking Style

MARY I. BERGER

Chicago

Orchard Books, Inc.

Fifth Edition

ISBN 0-9630778-0-5

Library of Congress Catalog Card Number 91-198147

The MOTHER GOOSE AND GRIMM comic strip is reprinted by permission: Tribune Media Services.

The SALLY FORTH comic strip is reprinted with special permission of North America Syndicate.

Thanks to Columbia College's Radio Department and Radio Station, WCRX, for the News, Sports, and Weather copy; the Commercial copy was adapted from coupon advertising; the public service announcement copy is original.

To
Edward, Ami and Daniel,
who pushed, teased and encouraged,

and

to
Al Parker,
who let me practice before I preached.

ACKNOWLEDGMENTS

I want first to acknowledge the hundreds of Columbia College students, as well as those private clients, who have worked so diligently and successfully to achieve bi-dialectalism. This book's content is a reflection of how much they have taught me about language differences. Their efforts solidified and validated the book's philosophy, method and materials; they are its inspiration.

It would have been impossible for me to have those students if it were not for Al Parker, Chairman of the Radio Department, Columbia College. I thank him again for giving me the courageous go-ahead to design and teach the course that served as the basis for the book.

Other than their disbelief in the need for appendices, Edward, Ami and Dan Berger were stalwart believers, and I give thanks for and to my family for their loving constancy.

I am indebted to Bonnie Oberman, my friend and editor, for her patience, advice and support; I could not have completed the book without her. I also send heartfelt thanks to cover artist Ron Boyd and to Josie Balinao for page layout and typography; and to Doris Handley, Natalie van Straaten, and Chitra Ragavan for their bits of wisdom, help and encouragement.

CONTENTS

One uses the language which helps to preserve one's life, which helps to make one feel at peace in the world, and which screens out the greatest amount of chaos. All human beings do this...

Show me how I can cling to that which is real to me, while teaching me a way into the larger society.

Ralph Ellison
September, 1963

INTRODUCTION

Linguists point out that languages and dialects contain features that are similar and different, not right or wrong. This manual's philosophy and methodology are based on that premise.

The goal of this manual is to help you to acquire the pronunciation and grammar of oral STANDARD ENGLISH (SE) so that you can compete effectively at school and at work. It is NOT the goal of this manual to replace the English dialect that you speak now. You should continue to use your style of English because it was the way you first expressed yourself; it binds you to your family, friends, neighborhood and region; it is an important link to your personal and cultural history.

If you do not speak SE, you need to learn it in addition to, not instead of, your own English dialect. If you are interested in an on-air career in broadcasting, you need to learn the GENERAL AMERICAN (GA) pronunciation system of SE presented in this manual. All of you will become BI-DIALECTIC, capable of speaking two dialects. You will be able to speak SE in school, at your professional work-place, and whenever you feel it would be beneficial to use it. You can use your primary dialect at home, with friends, and whenever you feel comfortable using it.

If you have a foreign-language background, this manual is intended to help you become more intelligible in English. It will enable you to REDUCE your ACCENT by presenting and contrasting many of the sounds and some of the grammatical structures of SE with those of your primary language.

Standard English: What It Is and What It Isn't

Standard English is the dialect of English that is spoken by those people who carry on the business and educational affairs of this country. SE has "official" recognition because grammar books and dictionaries have been written about its structure and pronunciation; whole expository works are written in its style. That is why the language conventions of SE are the most respected, emulated, and acceptable in our country.

It is important to recognize, however, that SE's acceptance is based on social prestige, and not on any natural linguistic superiority. SE is not an inherently better or worse system of communication than your dialect or any other systematic English dialect. Lorenzo D. Turner, William A. Stewart and J. L. Dillard, for example, are linguists who have conducted exhaustive scholarly research on an American English dialect called Black English (BE). Their research demonstrates that BE is as systematic and rule-governed in its pronunciation and grammar as SE.

It is equally important to remember that, just like SE, other dialects retain many of the phonetic and grammatical features of the African, Asian, and European languages from which they derived. For example, when SE speakers want to express past tense, they are emulating the style of the European languages from which their speaking style derives. When BE speakers want to express past tense, they are emulating the rules of the various West African languages from which BE derives. Both dialects can express the past; they just have different rules for how to do it.

You can see in the following examples that SE changes the verb to show the past and that BE uses a time-determiner word, like "yesterday," to express the past.

SE	BE
I walk to school.	I walk to school.
I walkED to school.	I walk to school YESTERDAY
Don WROTE me.	Don write me LAST MONDAY.

This Manual

This manual is divided into two sections: PRONUNCIATION DIFFERENCES and GRAMMATICAL DIFFERENCES. The lessons on pronunciation and grammar, as well as their respective drills and exercises, present DIFFERENCES and CONTRASTS, not "the right way" and "the wrong way." Each lesson contrasts a sound or grammatical feature of SE with the most common dialectic difference(s). The manual's method of presenting contrasting features helps to build awareness of your own features, which in turn enables you to identify the particular SE features you need to acquire.

As you identify these features, you may want to find out more about their derivations. For instance, YOUSE, as in YOUSE GUYS, comes from the Irish-Gaelic plural YOUS; the famous American Southern Y'ALL comes from the Scots-Irish and Appalachian translation of YOUS(E); the BE rule of emphasizing a sentence-subject with a pronoun, as in YOUR MOM, SHE'S SO PRETTY, comes from the West African languages. The sources of these examples and more information about the history of dialects can be found in the Notes and Sources section of the Appendix, and in the Bibliography.

The manual uses three labels for the dialect you are going to acquire for school, work and/or broadcasting:

STANDARD ENGLISH (SE) is the name of the most widely accepted and socially prestigious English dialect; it is used professionally and academically; it is no better or worse linguistically than any other rule-governed English dialect.

GENERAL AMERICAN (GA) is the preferred on-air SE dialect. The other two "standard" dialects are Southern SE and Eastern SE.

BROADCAST STYLE is the pronunciation style of General American.

First Things First: How to Use This Book

The first step in using this manual is NOT to use it yet! Begin your acquisition of oral SE by taping yourself in a ten-to-fifteen minute informal conversation, and while reading something out loud. Listen to the tape three times. Make a list of all the pronunciation and grammatical features in your dialect that differ from GA/SE. Write these features down on the next page.

BE ANALYTIC. Note sound-differences like DAT for THAT, FIRS for FIRST, and LOOKIN for LOOKING. Note word-choice contrasts, like WAS for WERE, YOUSE for YOU, and GOES for SAID. Note the omission of words such as IS and ARE.

After you complete your DIFFERENT FEATURES LIST, you are ready to begin to use the manual and the accompanying audio tape. Choose one feature from your list, find the appropriate lesson, and you are on your way to acquiring SE as an additional dialect. Note that letters enclosed in parentheses, for example (th) or (ile), represent the way sounds are PRONOUNCED, rather than the way words are spelled.

When you practice a new SE feature, ALWAYS CONTRAST it with an equivalent old (primary) feature. Contrasting the new with the old helps you to identify exactly what you feel and hear. The ease with which you can SWITCH from one dialect to another depends on your ability to recognize and consciously reproduce the differences.

Use the Appendix for supplemental drills and answers. Broadcasting students will find copy-samples of news, sports, commercials, weather, and P.S.A.s to practice.

Refer to the International Phonetic Alphabet (IPA), pages 147-149, for additional information regarding letter-sound differentiation and the General American/ Broadcast style of pronunciation. Your instructor may expect you to learn the IPA for your course work.

Finally, LEARN TO LISTEN. Listen to people who speak your dialect. Listen to people who speak General American Standard English. Listen to yourself. Analytic listening is always the best way to learn. Good luck!

Different Features List

Pronunciation Differences:

Grammatical Differences:

SECTION I: PRONUNCIATION DIFFERENCES

This section of the manual will help you to identify how your pronunciation of English differs from that of GA/SE speakers. The lessons will explain how to produce the GA/SE consonants and vowels. The lessons will also provide you with drills and exercises for contrast and practice.

Languages contain sounds that are both similar to and different from the sounds of other languages. When people come to the United States speaking a language/ dialect other than SE, they use their own systems of pronunciation (and grammar) when they speak English. For example, a person of Asian-Indian background might say VANT instead of WANT, and WERY instead of VERY, because in many Indian dialects, the letter "v" is pronounced like the SE (w) and vice versa.

Another common pronunciation difference is the reduction of a consonant cluster and/or the omission of a final consonant – like FIRS for FIRST, and HA for HAT. You might be interested to know that most Asian languages and many West African languages do not have words with final consonants, and have no consonant clusters. It isn't surprising, then, that people with these language backgrounds often reduce the consonant clusters and/or omit final consonants.

Your primary language SOUNDS and FEELS good. When you speak it, you feel comfortable – at home. When you are at school, at work, or in an interview, however, it is to your advantage to use SE pronunciation (and grammar).

As recommended in the Introduction, use your tape recorder to listen to yourself as you try to identify how your pronunciation differs from GA/SE. Continue using the tape recorder as you practice the new sounds because it is difficult to hear the differences while you are speaking.

Finally, remember to use the manual's method of contrasting the old with the new pronunciation so that you HEAR and FEEL the differences. Don't forget that the accompanying tape allows you to hear the differences.

Now, choose your first pronunciation difference, and begin.

Chapter 1: Consonant Clusters

A CONSONANT CLUSTER exists when two or more consonants are grouped together, like the (st) in BEST, and the (sps) in CLASPS. In Standard English, each consonant in the cluster must be pronounced, except in rare instances like the silent "gh" in THROUGH or HEIGHT, and the silent "p" in PSYCHOLOGY. The most common pronunciation difference occurs when the speaker reduces the consonant cluster by omitting one or more of the consonants, as in LEF for LEFT, or LIS for LISTS.

Test yourself on the following words. Do you pronounce the words in the SE column by producing each sound in the consonant cluster, or do you pronounce them as if they were the words in the DIFFERENCE column?

CLUSTER	SE	DIFFERENCE
nd	and	Ann
nd	mend	men
ft	deft	deaf
st	must	muss
st	missed	miss
sts	guests	guess (or) guest is
sk	mask	mass
sks	masks	mass (or) mask is
ld	cold	coal (or) code
ts	let's	less
cht	watched	watch
sp	grasp	grass
sps	wasps	wasp
sht	washed	wash
cht	reached	reach
nt	went	when
vd	lived	live
zd	dazed	daze
pt	tapped	tap
kt	knocked	knock
skt	risked	risk

The next several pages contain word drills that will help you master the pronunciation of SE consonant clusters. Before you begin each drill, note which sounds in the cluster you should hear and feel yourself producing. Then, make sure that you pronounce each sound, especially the sound that ends the cluster.

(nd) Cluster

The LAST SOUND you should hear and feel is (d). Note that past-tense words can also contain (nd) clusters.

and	mend	rained
band	send	dined
sand	lend	stained
stand	trend	loaned
mind	friend	trained
find	wand	groaned
kind	pond	gained
fiend	bond	signed

(ft) Cluster

The LAST SOUND you should hear and feel is (t). Note that past-tense words can also contain (ft) clusters.

left	raft	puffed
deft	shaft	stuffed
lift	theft	fluffed
gift	loft	coughed
soft	Taft	laughed
waft	bereft	golfed

(st) Cluster

The LAST SOUND you should hear and feel is (t). Note that past-tense words can also contain (st) clusters.

just	cast	missed
list	last	erased
rust	wrist	raced

(continued)

rest	arrest	faced
trust	boast	dressed
fast	best	announced
guest	waist	paced
nest	test	guessed
pest	chest	confessed
haste	paste	laced
worst	first	nursed
vest	haste	messed
west	east	leased

(nt), (pt) and (kt) Clusters

The LAST SOUND you should hear and feel is (t). Note that past-tense words can also contain the (pt) and (kt) clusters.

rent	shouldn't	kept	slapped	packed
went	wouldn't	leapt	stopped	faked
bent	couldn't	apt	napped	raked
meant	didn't	inept	act	liked
sent	aren't	rapt	fact	backed
tent	wasn't	dropped	pact	picked
can't	isn't	stepped	direct	tricked
won't	don't	ripped	indirect	ached
faint	musn't	drooped	perfect	worked

For more practice on "ed" word-endings, see pages 12-14.

(sp) and (sps) Clusters

The LAST SOUND you should hear and feel in words that end in (sp) is (p). When you add an (s), make sure you hear and feel the (ps) ending. See pages 27 and 30 for additional exercises.

grasp	wasp	grasps	wasps
lisp	rasp	lisps	rasps
clasp	gasp	clasps	gasps
wisp	cusp	wisps	cusps

(sk) and (sks) Clusters

The LAST SOUND you should hear and feel in words that end in (sk) is (k). When you add an (s), make sure you hear and feel the (ks) ending. See pages 10 and 27 for additional exercises.

ask	risk	asks	risks
task	bask	tasks	basks
mask	desk	masks	desks
disc	flask	discs	flasks
husk	cask	husks	casks
bisque	mosque	bisques	mosques

(sts) Cluster

The LAST TWO SOUNDS you should hear and feel are (ts) – not just (s) and not (tiz). For example, NESTS should end with (sssss-ts); it should not sound like NESS or NEST IS. See pages 26 and 27 for more drills.

nests	rests	casts
lists	wrists	mists
boasts	roasts	rusts
toasts	coasts	fasts
dusts	hosts	lusts
trusts	fists	masts

(ts) Cluster

The LAST TWO SOUNDS you should hear and feel are (ts), just like the last two sounds of the (sts) words. Remember, the word is LETS and not LESS. See pages 26-33 for additional exercises.

let's	it's	what's
that's	its	Pat's
boats	fits	cats
mats	mitts	rats

(mp), (mps) and (md) Clusters

Make sure you hear and feel the final sounds in these words. See pages 10, 12, and 27 for additional exercises.

stamp	stamps	rimmed
ramp	ramps	seemed
clamp	clamps	summed
stomp	stomps	roamed
romp	romps	tamed
dump	dumps	named
vamp	vamps	shamed
camp	camps	chimed
jump	jumps	rhymed
cramp	cramps	foamed
lamp	lamps	timed
limp	limps	combed

Practice Sentences with Capitalized Consonant Clusters

1. My frieND is so kiND that she fouND the perfeCT giFT aND I kePT it.
2. DoN'T aCT like a gueST. JuST make yourseLVeS coMFortable until you're relaXeD.
3. LiFT your leFT haND aND graSP the cluMP of daMP dirt until your haND feeLS craMPeD.
4. FirST, the bird flew eaST, then it flew weST to colleCT the sticKS for iTS neST.
5. They muST liST the reasoNS why they caN'T or woN'T atteND the laST meeting.
6. The men need to meND their socKS aND paNTS.
7. You muST not muss your dress when you're dresSED.
8. Tess's scores on her teSTS were excelleNT.
9. The gueSTS made guesses during charaDeS.
10. The Senior Class has piNS with diamoND claSPS.
11. GraSP each blade of grass in your haND.
12. LeT'S pay less money down to baNKS for loaNS.
13. LeT'S see if the baND leFT iTS instrumeNTS.

14. She truSTS PaT'S good sense about riSK-taking.

15. She pacKeD her baGS, waVeD, and walKeD out.

16. They leFT the diSCS on the toPS of their deSKS.

17. She aSKS her studeNTS to take professional riSKS.

18. DoN'T juST staND there – fiND a kiND frieND.

19. The neSTS were stufFeD with waSPS aND inseCTS.

20. He kePT the boaTS near the poSTS with roPeS.

(L) + Consonant

Make sure that you do not omit the (L) sound when it occurs before a consonant. (If you also have difficulty producing the (L) sound at the ends of words because you omit it, or substitute (o), see pages 36 and 54.) Test yourself by reading the following word-pairs. If they sound the same, you need to practice producing a strong (L) within the CONSONANT CLUSTER by raising your tongue for (L).

WORD-PAIR TEST

code............cold		rode............rolled	
sewed............sold		towed............told	
owed............old		cawed............called	
fought............fault		hawed............hauled	
hep............help		Maude............mauled	

In addition, be careful that you are also pronouncing the consonant that occurs AFTER the (L) so that GOLD and SOLD do not sound like GOAL and SOUL.

(L) Consonant Cluster Drill

hold	mold	gold
bold	cold	doled
fold	knolled	polled
rolled	sold	told
called	paled	sailed
nailed	bailed	failed
hailed	jailed	tailed
wailed	help	self
myself	itself	himself
ourselves	yourself	yourselves
themselves	shelf	shelves
Rudolph	wolf	wolves
golden	old	older
stalled	hauled	assault
salt	fault	Walter
vault	calls	falls
holes	rolls	goals
poles	souls	tails
also	always	almost
although	Althea	velvet

Practice Sentences with Capitalized (L) + Consonant Clusters

1. Be BoLD about foLDing the coLD water into the moLD.

2. His oLD goLD watch was haiLED as aLMost an antique.

3. HoLD on to your oLD goLD oLDSmobile.

4. WaLTer and ALTHea paLED when they were toLD they had faiLED the heaLTH course.

5. She aLWays soLD the veLVet dresses first.

6. Mr. CauLDer toLD me to heLP myseLF to his fiLES.

7. She caLLED the carpenter, waiLED at the cost for instaLLMent, naiLED the paintings to the waLLS herseLF, caLLED the carpenter and yeLLED, "I toLD you I would do it myseLF."

8. The beLLS aLWays toLLED at tweLVe in CharLESTon.

9. ALTHough he was oLDer than WaLTer, RudoLPH saiLED off to coLD war battLES around the worLD.

10. Every night at tweLVe, Mr. ReynoLDS roLLS out of bed, boiLS water and warms miLK for tea, fiLLS the bowLS of sugar, sets the oLD timer for his boiLED eggs, takes saLT down from the sheLVes, yeLLS to the newspaper delivery girLS, tastes the roLLS that are piLED high with coLD jam, whistLES for his goLDen Retriever, GoLDy, and boLDly walks out into the coLD.

11. My oLD car staLLED and I puLLED it home by myseLF.

12. The oLD woLVES foLDed their taiLS under their fiLLED stomachs, roLLED over, and howLED at the moon.

Ask - Axe Contrast

The most common difference in the pronunciation of ASK is to pronounce it as if it were AXE. The letter "x" is not a sound; it is the (ks) consonant cluster. When pronouncing AXE, the (k) comes before the (s); when pronouncing ASK in the SE style, the (s) comes before the (k). Try the following drills, making sure that you hear and feel the (s) before (k) at the appropriate times.

ssssk - ssssk - kssss - kssss - ssssk - ssssk

sk - sk - ks - ks - eesk - aaks - oosk - eeks

baSK - riSK - taSK - bacKS - tacKS - diSK - maSK

ASS-K   ASS-K   ASS-KS   ASS-KS   ASS-KT   ASS-KT

ASS-KING   ASS-KING   ASS-K   ASS-KS   ASS-KT   ASS-KING

ask......(ASS-K)	axe....(aks)
asks.....(ASS-KS)	axes...(aksiz)
asked....(ASS-KT)	axed....(akst)
asking...(ASS-KING)	axing...(aksing)

Practice Sentences with Capitalized Phonetic Spellings

1. I'll ASS-K my mother if I can go.

2. You ASS-K your mother, too.

3. He ASS-KS to go to the movies every Saturday.

4. Janie ASS-KS for a cookie.

5. Dan ASS-KT if he could watch TV.

6. Ami ASS-KT if she could stay in Boston.

7. Stop ASS-KING so many questions!

8. I always ASS-K if he sharpened his axe.

9. Paul ASS-KS me about our new axes.

10. Yesterday, I ASS-KT him if the logs were axed.

11. If the answer is "no," he's ASS-KING for an axing!

12. He ASS-KT me for my axe.

Practice Paragraphs for ASK

The following two paragraphs spell the ASK words phonetically. Try reading them out loud without thinking about the familiar spellings so that you accustom yourself to the new SE pronunciation.

My mother ASS-KS my brothers the same questions that my father ASS-KS them. Do you know what my parents ASS-K them? They ASS-K, "Did you ASS-K permission to play with your sister's toys. And did you ASS-K for those cookies?" Then, my mother ASS-KS, "Did you take a bath and wash with soap?" I always ASS-K my mother to stop ASS-KING those questions, because after she ASS-KS them about the bath, she remembers to ASS-K me the same question, and I hate to wash with soap!

One of the students ASS-KT the teacher a question. I didn't hear, so I ASS-KT the teacher to ASS-K the student to ASS-K the question again. The teacher said, "When you are ASS-KING a question, please ASS-K loudly so everyone can hear what you ASS-K." So, the student ASS-KT loudly enough for everyone to hear, and I didn't have to ASS-K what he ASS-KT.

Now, using SE pronunciation, read the same two paragraphs with the ASK words spelled in the usual manner. Tape record your reading so that you can determine which ASK words need more practice.

My mother asks my brothers the same questions that my father asks them. Do you know what my parents ask them? They ask, "Did you ask our permission to play with your sister's toys. And did you take a bath and wash with soap?" I always ask my mother to stop asking those questions, because after she asks them about the bath, she remembers to ask me the same questions, and I hate to wash with soap!

One of the students asked the teacher a question. I didn't hear, so I asked the teacher to ask the student to ask the question again. The teacher said, "When you are asking a question, please ask loudly so everyone can hear what you ask." So, the student asked loudly enough for everyone to hear, and I didn't have to ask what he asked.

"ed" Word-endings

If you tend to reduce consonant clusters and/or "ed" word-endings, make sure that you hear either (t) or (d) at the ends of the words in the first two columns. The third column lists words that end in "ed" but the endings are pronounced as (id), and are not consonant clusters.

(d)	(t)	(id)
loved	miffed	included
lived	laughed	graded
moved	staffed	faded
mobbed	ripped	stated
robbed	tapped	mated
lobbed	stopped	hated
stormed	wished	tasted
named	rushed	roasted
steamed	cashed	posted
rained	matched	wasted
loaned	munched	quoted
signed	watched	supported
amazed	missed	elected
raised	raced	dusted
seized	passed	rusted
changed	faced	appointed
arranged	laced	printed
managed	based	tinted
remembered	typed	hinted
stored	hoped	skated
shared	shaped	braided
rigged	liked	shaded
mugged	baked	paraded
lugged	cooked	corroded
mailed	risked	added
sailed	asked	divided
nailed	picked	united
bathed	walked	initiated

(d)	(t)	(id)
enjoyed	talked	intended
cried	fished	offended
played	patched	defended
snowed	mashed	lasted

The following words contain additional consonant clusters that are "ed" endings. When you practice them, make sure that you hear and feel the final (t) and (d) sounds.

(bd)	(njd)	(thd)	(sht)
grabbed	changed	bathed	washed
stabbed	arranged	writhed	brushed
lobbed	deranged	soothed	hushed
nabbed		tithed	cashed
rehabbed	**(vd)**	clothed	lashed
	waved	loathed	
(gd)	staved	breathed	**(cht)**
lagged	raved	smoothed	lunched
flagged	halved		ditched
flogged	saved	**(zd)**	pitched
rigged	paved	advised	hatched
hugged	arrived	raised	bleached
	caved	gazed	perched
(jd)	survived	dazed	touched
aged	dived	eased	lurched
caged	waved	amazed	reached
judged	slaved	glazed	hitched
charged	braved		latched
raged	shaved	**(pst)**	
	jived	lapsed	
	craved	collapsed	
		elapsed	

Practice Sentences with Capitalized "ed" Endings

1. She dressED herself, then chargED what she purchasED.
2. She lovED the house in which her parents had livED.
3. He lobbED the ball and robbED Ted of the point.
4. Pete was amazED that he had raisED enough money.
5. We watchED the game and munchED chips and popcorn.
6. He was impressED that she walkED ten miles.
7. We huggED and kissED our daughter when she arrivED.
8. Ami studiED hard, typED three papers and earnED an A.
9. Dan dribblED the ball, fakED the shot and passED.
10. He climbED the tree, then jumpED to the ground.
11. John hirED him, noticED he was lazy and firED him.
12. He hammerED and nailED and sawED until he finishED.
13. Mary lacED up her shoes, then racED to the finish.
14. He arrangED the flowers and placED them on a table.
15. I cookED the dinner and bakED dessert for the party.
16. He was pickED last but playED the best.
17. We walkED and talkED and stoppED for ice cream.
18. He riskED all his savings and wagerED a bet.
19. Joe darnED his own socks, and patchED his jeans.
20. She practicED and rehearsED and achievED perfection.
21. She askED if he had pickED the winner yet.
22. She was thrillED when told she had earnED a prize.
23. The bank loanED the money then askED for it back.
24. The wolf huffED and puffED and demolishED the house.

(shtr) - (str) Contrast

A common pronunciation difference is the substitution of (sh) for (s) in the (str) cluster. In Broadcast/Standard English style, (str) must begin with an (s) sound, not an (sh) sound. Read the following nonsense syllables and words, making sure that you are pronouncing an (s), NOT an (sh), at the beginning or in the middle of each syllable. You should feel your lips smiling for (s) rather than "pooching" for (sh).

s-tra	s-tre	s-tri	s-tro	s-tru
strow	straw	struh	strim	strov
estri	ostra	ustru	astro	istre

stray	streak	straddle
straggle	straight	strain
strand	strange	stranger
strangle	strap	strategy
straw	strawberry	stream
streamlined	street	strength
strenuous	stress	stretch
strict	strident	strike
string	stripe	strong
structure	struggle	strum
strut	strychnine	stroll
instruct	destruct	construct
instructor	destruction	constructive
astronomy	astrology	distress
pastrami	gastric	distressful
mistress	maestro	restrain

Practice Sentences with Capitalized (s) – not (sh) – Sounds

1. My aStronomy inStructor reStricts studying aStrology.

2. The Stress and Struggle of life is diStressful.

3. Strong String is needed to conStruct the Structure.

4. Sunday Strollers Strutted by, eating Strawberries.

5. The arsonist deStroyed the reStructured diStrict.

6. MiStress Mary inStructs others not to eat paStrami.

7. A reStricted diet is worth the Struggle for reStraint.

8. Strong Stretching encourages Strength.

Medial Consonant Clusters: kYOU and gYOU

SE pronunciation insists that the speaker pronounce both consonants in the middle of words like PARTICULAR and REGULAR. Pronunciation differences occur when (uh) is substituted for YOU. For example:

	SE	**DIFFERENCE**
PARTICULAR	par-tih-kYOU-ler	par-tick-uh-ler
REGULAR	reh-gYOU-ler	reg-uh-ler

Practice Words Emphasizing Medial YOU

particular	(par tih kYOU ler)
accurate	(a kYOUR it)
ridiculous	(ruh dih kYOU liss)
vehicular	(vuh hih kYOU ler)
curriculum	(ker ih kYOU lum)
jocular	(jah kYOU ler)
Mercury	(mer kYOU ree)
meticulous	(meh tih kYOU luss)
matriculate	(ma trih kYOU late)
muscular	(muss kYOU ler)
reticular	(reh tih kYOU ler)
executive	(egg zeh kYOU tiv)
regularly	(reh gYOU lair lee)
argument	(ar gYOU ment)
irregular	(ear reh gYOU ler)
jugular	(juh gYOU ler)
coagulate	(co a gYOU late)

Practice Sentences with Capitalized kYOU and gYOU Sounds

1. The curriCUlum about MerCUry is partiCUlarly difficult.
2. She is an acCUrate student, but she is arGUmentative.
3. ReGUlar attendance is partiCUlarly important.
4. MetiCUlous attention to detail is an exeCUtive trait.
5. MusCUlar bodies are often joCUlar to see.

6. I matriCUlated, then I chose my curriCUlar major.

7. He uttered inacCUracies with reGUlarity.

8. ExeCUtives reGUlarly go after competitors' juGUlars.

9. Be metiCUlous and acCUrate when taking notes.

10. It's ridiCUlous to arGUe reGUlarly.

11. This curriCUlum is partiCUlarly difficult.

12. Policemen check for vehiCUlar irreGUlarities.

Medial Consonant Clusters: (ks), (gz), (gj) and (gn)

SE speakers usually pronounce all consonants that occur in the middle of words (see page 16). X, XC and CC are pronounced as (ks); if (h) or a vowel sound follows the X, then it is pronounced as (gz). Both consonants in the GG and GN clusters are pronounced. The most common pronunciation difference from SE is omission of (k) and (g) from these consonant clusters. For example:

	SE	DIFFERENCE
EXPECT	eks pekt	eh spekt
EXIST	egg zist	eh zist
SUCCESS	suck sess	suh sess
SUGGEST	sug jest	suh jest
RECOGNIZE	rek ug nize	rek uh nize

Practice the following words and sentences, making sure that you feel and hear BOTH consonants in the cluster.

(ks)

excellent	excite
except	expect
explain	exclamation
excel	excluded
experience	extension
exterior	external
expose	exquisite
expressive	expand
extraordinary	extra
expect	expose
success	successful
accent	accented
accept	acceptable
eccentric	eccentricity

(gz)

exhilarate	exhume
exaggerate	exert
exist	exile
exigency	exertion
exact	exhibit
exacerbate	exit
exorbitant	exited
exodus	exult
executive	exhort
existential	exiting

(gn)

recognition	recognize
recognizing	recognized

(gj)

suggestive	suggested
suggestion	suggest

Practice Sentences with Capitalized Medial Clusters

1. The eXCellent suGGestion eXhilarated his suCCessor.
2. The eCCentric eXhibited an eXpressive aCCent.
3. His eXtraordinary eXperiences eXpanded his eXistence.
4. Jane's eXorbitance eXposed an eXodus of eXecutives.
5. EXCitement pervaded the eXquisite eXhibit.
6. I aCCept the suGGestion that we eXit eXactly at six.
7. ECCentrics suCCeed in eXhorting us to eXperiment.
8. It's aCCeptable to eXaggerate eXact eXpectation.
9. Laura recoGNized and aCCepted Tom's eCCentricities.
10. Carol recoGNizes that her aCCent is aCCeptable.
11. He suGGested a recoGNition award for eXCellence.
12. EXpect to be visually eXCited by the house's eXterior.
13. She was eXpected to recoGNize siXteen eXamples of foreign aCCents.
14. All of his eXCellent and eXtraordinary eXperiences suGGested that he was an aCCeptable candidate for the job of eXcursion guide.
15. AleXis and MaXine eXCitedly eXplained why they had eXited the party so eXpeditiously.
16. Don't eXacerbate your money situation by spending eXorbitantly and eXpanding your debt.
17. RecoGNizing eXquisite work is eXhilarating.
18. When the eXhumed body was eXhibited, everyone eXited.
19. She eXerted the eXpected energy and was aCCepted as an eXecutive.
20. MaXamillian aCCepted his eXpanding waistline as an eXCellent eXterior improvement; MaXine, his wife, recoGNized that his waist's eXtension was not aCCeptable, and strongly eXhorted him to eXert eXtensive energy into eXercising.

Chapter 2: Consonant Sounds

VOICED and VOICELESS Consonant-Pairs:

(d) - (t)	**(b) - (p)**	**(g) - (k)**	**(th) - (th)**
(z) - (s)	**(v) - (f)**	**(j) - (ch)**	**(zh) - (sh)**

Each of the consonant-pairs listed above consists of a voiced and voiceless sound. The first sound of each pair is VOICED, meaning that SOUND occurs in addition to the other features that it shares with its pair. You can FEEL the VIBRATION of the vocal cords that produces the sound by placing your hand lightly on your throat; you can hear the vibration as a HUM that accompanies production of the consonant.

The second sound of each pair is VOICELESS. It is produced by emitting a puff of air (t, p, k, ch) or stream of air (s, sh, th, f). You should not feel any vibration or hear any hum when you produce the voiceless sounds.

THE SOUNDS OF EACH PAIR ARE PRODUCED EXACTLY ALIKE EXCEPT FOR THE VOICING FEATURE. Voicing is important to being understood. For example, if you say BUCK for BUG, or ROPE for ROBE, you may not be understood. It is very possible that you do not differentiate between some of these consonant pairs if English is not your primary language.

Read the following word-pairs aloud. Make sure that you hear the hum and feel vibration for the voiced sounds; you should hear only air streaming or puffing out for the voiceless sounds.

(d)	**(t)**	**(b)**	**(p)**	**(g)**	**(k)**	**(v)**	**(f)**
duh	tuh	buh	puh	guh	kuh	vvvv	ffff
do	to	been	pin	got	cot	vat	fat
den	ten	bun	pun	goat	coat	veil	fail
bad	bat	lobe	lope	dug	duck	leave	leaf
had	hat	mob	mop	wig	wick	have	half
raid	rate	cob	cop	mug	muck	save	safe

(z)	(s)	(j)	(ch)	Voiced (th)	Voiceless (th)	(zh)
zzzz	ssss	juh	chuh	ththth	ththth	zhzhzh
zip	sip	jaw	chaw	thy	thigh	treasure
zag	sag	gyp	chip	this'll	thistle	measure
eyes	ice	ridge	rich	either	ether	leisure
phase	face	Madge	match	teethe	teeth	pleasure
rise	rice	gin	chin	wreathe	wreath	fusion

Note the following:
- When "t" occurs in the middle of words, it is often pronounced as a (d), as in BUTTER.
- "s" is often pronounced as a (z) when it is: between two vowels, as in EASY; at the ends of words, after vowels and voiced consonants, as in SAYS and FADS.
- "f" is pronounced as a (v) in the word OF.
- The "ed" ending is pronounced as a (t), (d), or (id). See page 12 for a more detailed explanation.

Practice Sentences with VOICED Consonants Capitalized

1. BoB loVeS THe feel oF soft leaTHer on hiS hanDS.
2. THe roBBer took eVerything THat waS oF Value to Grace.
3. John neVer Guessed THat Gale haD loVeD him for yearS.
4. TreaSUre THoSe DayS THat Bring you Joy anD loVe.
5. WiVeS, rememBer to huG your chilDren, huSBanD anD DoG.
6. She likes kinD anD tenDer men, not Bossy Cross oneS.
7. Jackie is maJoring in EnGlish, JournaliSm and parTying.
8. It's BeTTer to haVe loVeD anD lost THan neVer to haVe loVeD at all.
9. NeVer chanGe your real self Just BecauSe oTHerS suGGest THat you're not GooD enough aS you alreaDy are.
10. MeaSure success By your accomplishments, not By money.
11. He walked out oF her house and neVer looked Back.
12. RoBert anD LiZZy moVeD to a liTTle VillaGe anD liVeD toGeTHer in a farmhouse with caTTle in THe Back yarD.
13. She'S tireD oF THe noiSe anD THe ruDeness oF THe ciTy.
14. MrS. ToBin reSigneD aS PreSiDent oF THe BoarD oF THe VolunteerS for BeTTer eDucation.

(th) Sounds:

Voiced (th) Sound

The voiced (th) sound is produced by biting down gently on your tongue while humming. This results in a mild vibration or ticklish feeling on your tongue. The most common difference in pronunciation is producing a (d) instead of the voiced (th) sound. First, test yourself on the following word-pairs to see if they sound the same or different. Practice them until you are sure that the voiced (th) words sound and feel like a (th), not a (d) sound.

den - then	fodder - father
duh! - the	mutter - mother
dare - there, their, they're	letter - leather
day - they	wetter - weather
doe - though	eater - either
Dan - than	kneader - neither
(dat) - that	all dough - although
doe - though	breed - breathe
(dem) - them	load - loathe
utter - other	bade - bathe
an udder - another	seed - seethe

Word-Pair Practice Sentences

1. She paused, and THEN she went into the DEN.
2. "DUH!" said THE dumb cartoon character.
3. THEY like the DAY, but they LOATHE to LOAD hay.
4. DAN likes the night better THAN the day.
5. ALL DOUGH should be refrigerated, ALTHOUGH some isn't.
6. DEE'S children are THESE kids.
7. DARE me to take away THEIR toys.
8. My MOTHER doesn't like us to MUTTER.
9. My FATHER takes care of the FODDER on the farm.
10. We'll get much WETTER in this WEATHER.
11. She BADE him to BATHE daily.
12. That BREED of dog does not BREATHE well.

Voiceless (th) Sound

The voiceless (th) sound is produced by biting down gently on your tongue while soundlessly hissing out air. The most common pronunciation differences are producing (t) or (f) instead of the voiceless (th) sound. First, test yourself on the following word-triplets to determine if any differences in pronunciation exist. Then, practice the word list until you are sure that you can produce the voiceless (th) when required.

V-less (th)	(t)	(f)
with	wit	whiff
Ruth	root	roof
Ruth's	roots	roof's
death	debt	deaf
oath	oat	oaf
hath	hat	half
sheath	sheet	sheaf
myth	mitt	miff
myths	mitts	miffs
ruthless	rootless	roofless

If you have discovered that you substitute (f) for voiceless (th), it is likely that you do so when voiceless (th) occurs in the middle or final position of words, and not at the beginning. If, however, you substitute (t) for voiceless (th), it is possible that you do so in every word position. **Practice the following word list and make sure you are feeling and hearing the voiceless (th).**

think	with	without
thought	health	healthy
Thursday	birth	birthday
thank you	length	lengthy
thing	tooth	toothbrush
thick	bath	bathroom
third	math	mathematical
thirsty	faith	faithful
thousand	worth	worthless
thin	breath	breathtaking
three	month	monthly
thirty	mouth	mouthful

(continued)

thunder	wrath	author
thelma	seventh	method
thirteen	ninth	anything
thigh	youth	nothing
thorn	truth	truthful
thumb	north	northwest

Practice Sentences with Capitalized VOICED and VOICELESS (th) Sounds

1. THis is THe
smallest
biggest
oldest book in THe room.
THickest
THinnest

2. THese are THe
blue
green
yellow chairs and tables.
orange
purple

3. THose are my
moTHer's
faTHer's
grandmoTHer's shoes.
grandfaTHer's
broTHer's

4. THey like THeir
hamburgers
hot dogs
chicken wiTH fries.
egg salad
tuna fish

5. THat is her
belt
dog
house over THere.
sister
friend

6. My birTHday is
April 25TH.
March 4TH.
January 19TH.
September 6TH.
November 30TH (THirtieTH).

AlTHea	*5TH*
ArTHur	*7TH*

7. I'm in maTH class wiTH   *DoroTHy*   during   *8TH*   period.
LuTHer	*10TH*
CaTHy	*9TH*

norTH
souTH

8. I live   norTHeast   of RuTH's house.
   souTHwest
   norTHwest

Practice Sentences with Capitalized VOICED and VOICELESS (th) Sounds

1. THere are THose who always THink someTHing is wrong.

2. THank you for all THese birTHday presents.

3. BeTH's moTHer was THe THinnest and THe healTHiest.

4. Take your washcloTH and tooTHbrush into THe baTHroom.

5. THat sevenTH maTH problem was too lengTHy for me.

6. I THought you became THirty last THursday.

7. ArTHur and CaTHy live norTHeast of RuTH and LuTHer.

8. THe healTH of THe earTH depends on our faiTHful care.

9. THrow THree balls THrough THe hoop and you win.

10. We can do wiTHout wealTH but we cannot do wiTHout love.

11. THe ninTH youTH in line wins a THick milkshake.

12. She took an oaTH to be truTHful, but it was worTHless.

13. ElizabeTH blew out THe THirteen candles on her cake.

14. My grandmoTHer and grandfaTHer had a fiftieTH wedding anniversary and we surprised THem wiTH a party.

15. THe breaTHtaking view left THem momentarily breaTHless.

16. THe paTH THat led to THeir house was not smooTH.

17. THat's THe fourTH time THeir team lost THe game.

18. THree THousand dollars is a lot of money for THat job.

19. THere's someTHing THat I'd like you to do for THem.

20. FifTH-ranked DePaul beat MonmouTH College THirteen to THree.

21. THe Cubs out-scored THe Mets THirty-THree to noTHing.

22. Inflation rose faster in THe NorTHeast THan in THe souTHern part of THe country.

(s) and (z) Sounds

If English is not your primary language, you may substitute the (s) sound for the (z) sound. Many languages, including most dialects of Spanish, do not include (z) in their phonetic systems. The (z) sound is produced the same way as (s), except that (z) is VOICED and makes a "buzzy" sound rather than the voiceless hiss produced by (s). Note that "s" spellings are often pronounced as (z) sounds, when they occur between vowels and after voiced consonants. (See page 20 for more exercises on Voiced-Voiceless sounds.)

Practice the following word-pairs, making sure that you hear and feel a "buzzy" voiced sound for (z).

(s)	(z)	(s)	(z)	(s)	(z)
sip	zip	racing	raising	price	prize
seek	Zeke	bussing	buzzing	peace	peas
Sue	zoo	maces	mazes	base	bays
sink	zinc	racer	razor	ice	eyes
singer	zinger	doses	dozes	sauce	saws
see	Zee	lacy	lazy	dice	dies
simmer	Zimmer	ricing	rising	hiss	his

Practice Sentences with Capitalized (z) Sounds

1. It's not eaSy to uSe a raZor the first ten timeS.
2. Sue sawS the logS and giveS Tim thoSe that are hiS.
3. SuSan noticeS that Dan studieS alone while most kidS study in groups.
4. LaZy dogS alwayS lie near open sunny doorwayS.
5. He waS reSistant to change, but she iS flexible.
6. She met preSidents, senatorS and repreSentativeS.
7. DoeS DaiSy like to ski and skate or iS she scared?
8. Sally waS eager to get A'S and B'S on her eXamS.
9. ReaSons were given aS to why laSer beamS work.
10. Overuse of computerS tendS to make us diZZy.

"s" Word-endings

Many Asian and African languages do not need word endings to express the four concepts discussed below. Nor is it necessary for some English dialects that are derived from those languages to add "s." For example, BE shows plurality and possession by placing number-words and possessor-words next to the noun. BE does not need the third person "s" ending because its present tense verb endings do not change; it rarely needs contractions, because it omits the connecting be-verbs (see pages 86 and 88). Here are the four instances where Broadcast/Standard English adds "s" to the ends of words:

1. To pluralize: I have four bookS.

2. To mark possession: Jane'S book is sad.

3. To mark third person singular present tense:

   He hitS the ball. NaShawn readS long books. It feelS smooth. She haS one. Mark likeS her.

4. To contract IS and HAS:

   She'S pretty. He'S busy. The dog'S barking. Tom'S been busy. Sally'S left work.

Read the following sentence-pairs to determine which "s" endings you use or omit:

1. I saw all Kareem kid and one son look like Kareem.
   I saw all Kareem'S kidS and one son lookS like Kareem.

2. He have ten cent to lend to Sam brother.
   He haS ten centS to lend to Sam'S brother.

3. She happy that Aisha sweater fit her, too.
   She'S happy that Aisha'S sweater fitS her, too.

4. Dan radio work, but it make a lot of static.
   Dan'S radio workS, but it makeS a lot of static.

5. It nice and warm outside, but Lisa been inside.
   It'S nice and warm outside, but Lisa'S been inside.

Remember: "s" word-endings are sometimes prounounced as (s), and sometimes pronouned as (z). See pages 20 and 26 for more information and drills regarding these two sounds.

Following are explanations, drills and practice sentences regarding the four SE instances when "s" must be added to the ends of words.

Plural "s" Word-endings

Broadcast/Standard English usually shows plurality (more than one) by adding "**s**" to the end of the noun. For example: I have one friend. You have two friends. There are two exceptions to this rule. The first exception is illustrated by words that change in spelling to show plurality. For example:

<table>
<tr><td>1 foot - 2 feet</td><td>1 tooth - 6 teeth</td></tr>
<tr><td>1 child - 3 children</td><td>1 man - 7 men</td></tr>
<tr><td>1 mouse - 4 mice</td><td>1 goose - 8 geese</td></tr>
<tr><td>1 woman - 5 women</td><td>1 die - 9 dice</td></tr>
</table>

The second exception is illustrated by those words which do NOT change to show plurality:

<table>
<tr><td>1 sheep - 13 sheep</td><td>1 piece of ice - a lot of ice</td></tr>
<tr><td>1 fish - lots of fish</td><td>1 piece of beef - some beef</td></tr>
<tr><td>1 deer - many deer</td><td>1 of you - all of you</td></tr>
</table>

Most of our other nouns need "**s**" endings to show that we are talking about more than one of something. Practice the following list of words, making sure that you are hearing, feeling and seeing the "**s**" word-endings; put each word into a sentence.

fingers	toes	eyes	legs
cents	dollars	stores	kids
tables	chairs	arms	seats
couches	lunches	guesses	dances
ranches	glasses	brains	trains
songs	rings	kings	stings
desks	tasks	masks	mops
wasps	grapes	tapes	capes
hats	cats	mitts	lists
masts	hosts	casts	baths
cloths	moths	months	tons
games	limes	bills	sales

There are more word lists on pages 4, 5 and 6 that focus on difficult consonant clusters ending in "**s.**"

Possessive "s" Word-endings

SE shows singular possession by adding **'s**, and plural possession by adding **s'** to the ends of words. For example:

> The dog's tail is wagging.
>
> The girls' dresses are pretty.
>
> The purse's two zippers are broken.

If your style of speaking English does not usually make use of the possessive *"s"* word-ending, then you probably use one or both of the following language differences:

1. OMISSION of the possessive *"s"*:

> Jane sister was sick.
>
> John brother is nice.
>
> That man voice is annoying.
>
> The dog tail is short.

2. ADDITION OF *"s"* or (n) to SE pronouns that already show possession.

> That apple is mines.
>
> The book is his'n.

Practice the following word list, making sure that you hear and feel yourself using the possessive *"s"* word-endings.

girl's sweater	man's door	boy's job
dog's fur	zoo's cages	mother's work
dad's tools	teacher's job	house's rooms
students' pens	spoon's handle	job's salary
John's son	Jean's sister	Mary's mother
Dan's father	lions' manes	worker's drill

Sentences with Capitalized Possessive "s" Word-endings

1. Dan'S father and Mary'S mother are in the den.

2. The girl'S sweater has the dog'S fur all over it.

(continued)

3. The boy'S job was to clean the zoo'S cages.

4. John'S son cleaned the house'S rooms.

5. None of Dad'S tools could repair the spoon'S handle.

6. Jean'S sister did not want to brush the lion'S mane.

7. The workerS' drills broke on the hard wooden floor.

8. The student'S pens were left at his friend'S house.

Third Person Singular Present Tense "s" Word-endings

SE insists that you add an "s" to the end of third person singular present tense verbs in order for the subject and verb to agree. Read the following sentence-pairs and try to determine if you use or omit this type of "s" verb-ending:

He walk to school.   She run faster.   It seem warm.

HE walkS to school.   SHE runS faster.   IT seemS warm.

John need a job.   College have its advantages.

John needS a job.   College haS its advantage.

Use the following verb conjugation chart to review what we mean by third person singular present tense.

	PRESENT TENSE	
	SINGULAR	PLURAL
First person	I have	We have
Second person	You have	You have
THIRD PERSON	HE, SHE, IT HAS	They have

Third person also refers to all the nouns that HE, SHE and IT represent. For example:

The boy (HE) drives to work.   John (HE) writes well.

Jennifer (SHE) likes school.   My mom (SHE) is tall.

The radio (IT) is broken.   School (IT) is fun.

Note which verbs need "s" endings in the following sentences:

1. If he break the radio, we'll miss the game. (breaks)

2. She like to dance when she goes to parties. (likes)

3. Tom think he need to write his paper. (thinks, needs)

4. We think he can wait until tomorrow. (none)

5. I like the way my dog jump for his ball. (jumps)

Note the "s" endings of verbs in the following sentences:

1. Our cat loves to jump on the furniture.

2. John says that he gets tired when he lifts weights.

3. Her teacher knows that not everyone likes math.

4. Anyone who does not read this chapter stays late.

5. She does the laundry, sweeps the floors and cooks.

6. It seems odd that she works and he stays at home.

7. When my dad saves money, he always buys us presents.

8. My teacher never praises me when she reads my papers.

Read the following sentences. Change the word I to HE or SHE and add the "s" ending to the appropriate verb. Then change the I to a personal name, again making the appropriate verb-ending changes. For example:

> I write many letters every day.
> HE writeS many letters every day.
> SAM writeS many letters every day.

1. I read all the important letters.

2. I always type the reports carefully.

3. I never make mistakes.

4. I don't have a private secretary.

5. I usually work in the main office.

6. I meet all the important visitors.

7. I get the information from Ms. Smith.

8. I never send the reports to Mr. Johnson.

(continued)

9. I answer the important memos.

10. I rarely talk to Smith and Johnson.

11. I usually like my job.

12. I sometimes get tired and then I rest.

13. I never drink coffee or coke.

14. I always insist on punctuality.

15. I never smoke at my desk.

Make whatever changes are necessary so that the following sentences contain third person singular present tense verbs:

1. He scare me when he make that ugly face.

2. She talk too loudly and the teacher get mad.

3. Whenever he go to school the bell ring too early.

4. The TV never seem to work when "L.A. Law" go on.

5. That girl live in a house on Elm Street.

6. She brush her hair every night for ten minutes.

7. He miss his family when he go to camp.

8. Janie read one chapter nightly when she go to bed.

Make the necessary SE third person singular present tense verb-ending changes to the following story:

"My boss love it when she know I've made a mistake. She tell me that I'm a good worker but she correct me all the time. For instance, when she first come into the office and look at me, she say, 'Good morning, Mary.' But then she always say, 'Please get off of the phone, now.' Then, when she check my work she usually say, 'This letter look pretty good, Mary, but it do need retyping.' Sometimes, she call me into her office and ask me to get some coffee. That only bother me if I'm busy retyping the letter."

Third Person Singular Present Tense "s" Contractions

SE speakers often contract the words IS and HAS into "s" word-endings. For example, "she'S going home" and "he'S been there" are used more often than "she is going home" or "he has been there." Omission of the "s" word-endings as contractions is a common speech difference. Read the following sentence-pairs and determine if you are omitting the "s" word-endings when the contractions are necessary in order for the sentence to have a SE verb.

She happy.	He tired.	She pretty.	He tall.
She's happy.	He's tired.	She's pretty.	He's tall.

He gone home.	Tom done his paper.	She been away.
He's gone home.	Tom's done his paper.	She's been away.

Read the following practice sentences, making sure that you feel and hear the capitalized "s" word-endings that are contractions for IS and HAS.

1. It'S not too late to go out but he'S left already.
2. She'S not the one who paid for you.
3. The librarian'S getting the book for me.
4. The secretary'S typing the letter.
5. I'm sorry, but the computer'S down.
6. I'll call you back when it'S not so busy.
7. Rasheed'S going to call so I better get off.
8. Ayanna'S been away for a week and she'S called once.
9. Eduardo'S not gone to work for a long time.
10. He'S a doctor and she'S a veterinarian.
11. It'S a shame that she'S not graduating.
12. Bonnie'S so excited about her new furniture and floor.
13. The last one in the water'S a rotten egg.
14. He'S so handsome but he'S a fool.
15. Who'S going to volunteer to make the salad?

(continued)

16. Janie'S always a good sport when she loses.

17. She'S always happy and he'S always sad.

18. The dog'S barking because he'S hungry.

19. The kitty'S meowing because she'S scared.

20. This room'S the same color as the kitchen.

21. Your sunburn'S peeling.

22. My aunt'S coming to the graduation.

23. Rashard'S really angry that Beth'S not home.

24. The printer'S broken and my paper'S due today.

25. The teller'S ignoring the guard'S scream.

"s" Word-ending Practice Sentences

1. My sister's piggy bank has 20 dollars and 35 cents.

2. She's the best batter and he's the best pitcher.

3. Her mother's best friends gave her some new tapes.

4. The zoo-keeper's favorite gorilla's been sick.

5. Thousands of wasps caused hundreds of stings.

6. He continues to take ridiculous risks.

7. He fails to impress his manager's bosses.

8. Sarah wishes for new dresses for her dolls.

9. My husband's employer buys him breakfasts and lunches.

10. She goes to her brother's store and works every day.

11. Yukimi's bracelets always fall off her wrists.

12. She's already washed the dishes and glasses.

13. In six months Dantrell's going to earn two college degrees.

14. Sometimes, Dan doesn't do his teachers' assignments.

15. The coach tells him to lift weights, but he forgets.

16. The United States of America elects its presidents.

17. Politicians' promises are worthless memories.

18. The computer needs new programs to stay modern.

19. Mothers' worries usually are about their children.

20. Feet need comfortable shoes and socks for protection.

21. He looks at his lists to remind him of his chores.

22. She reads and memorizes five books every two months.

23. The radio breaks down and Tom always fixes it.

24. Sam sweeps and mops and washes the dishes every night.

25. The President's advisors alwasy prepare him for press conferences on Tuesdays.

26. Sometimes, Chicago's beaches are closed because the city's health inspector finds samples of bacteria.

27. She's the one who has to entertain visiting dignitaries on Thursdays.

28. Darrell's the man who judges the students' science projects.

29. Claudia's never seen Rome's seven hills and hundreds of monuments.

30. When Matt debates, he walks around, screams and shakes his fists at his opponents.

31. When Daniel debates, he recites facts and figures so his opponent thinks that he knows everything about his topics.

32. When Angie debates, she frowns, paces and intimidates anyone who thinks he can produce rebuttals.

33. Mary wishes that her students would pay more attention to their speeches and exams than to their friends and parties.

34. Rex's dogs and cats sleep on his house's couches and chairs.

35. Pens, pencils, notebooks and computers are the necessities of students' lives.

36. John never finds what he's looking for without his glasses.

37. Danita always has her books and assignments for classes.

38. Katherine continues to excel in her studies.

39. Roger never prepares his audiotapes for his radio classes.

40. Dwayne knows that if he practices and practices, he will hear changes in his speech.

41. The teacher's standards for grades are relative to each student's efforts and the consequences of those efforts.

42. She earns mostly B's and C's, but the last two semesters' grades have been all A's.

43. Meggie always throws herself against the door, then leaps down the stairs, barks wildly, and jumps in circles when Lulu walks by the house.

44. Lulu just looks at Meggie and keeps on trotting.

45. Meggie's a Wheaten Terrier and Lulu's a Standard Poodle.

Final (L) Sound

Most of you already make an acceptable (L) at the beginning of words, and when the (L) is between two vowels in the middle of words. For example, the (L) in LOOK and ALIVE are probably easy for you to produce. The most common pronunciation difference regarding (L) is omission of the (L) when it occurs in the final position of a word and before a consonant. We have already presented a drill (on page 8) for the production of (L) in consonant cluster words like OLD and CHILD. Now, test yourself on the following word-pairs. Do you raise your tongue at the end of the word and produce (L), or do you omit (L) as in BAW for BALL, or substitute (o) for (L) as in RIDDO for RIDDLE?

OMISSION or (o)	(L)
aw	all
go	goal
to	tool
stew	stool
rue	rule
Phoo	fool
ow	owl
caw	call
hoe	hole
row	role
lid oh	little
mid oh	middle
rid oh	riddle
Roy oh	royal
he oh	he'll
she oh	she'll
few owe	fuel
you owe	you'll
I owe	I'll

In order to produce an acceptable (L) at the ends of words, your tongue must be moving up while you vocalize. Make sure that you feel, hear and see the (L) at the ends of the words in the following drill.

ill	call	sale	mile	hole
fill	ball	tale	tile	role
still	fall	male	style	pole

will	all	fail	file	goal
hill	wall	nail	dial	bowl
chill	hall	rail	guile	soul
seal	fowl	boil	pal	pull
meal	howl	toil	gal	full
real	towel	oil	Hal	bull
feel	bowel	foil	Cal	wool
he'll	owl	spoil	shall	
she'll	Powell	soil		

tool	lapel	little
cool	dispel	riddle
school	repel	fiddle
rule	spell	rattle
jewel	Mel	saddle
fool	fell	cattle

Practice Sentences with Final (L) Facilitated by Initial (L)

The following sentences contain two-word phrases that allow you to use your already-established production of the (L) that begins words, in order to help you to produce the word-ending (L) sound. Produce the two-word (L) phrases, CALL ON and FELL OVER, as if they were one word with an (L) sound in the middle, as in CALLON and FELLOVER.

1. WILL OUR kids CALL ON our new neighbor today?
2. FILL OUT this application.
3. PULL OVER before we have an accident.
4. CALL OUT your first name when I say your number.
5. She brought a PAIL OF water from the beach.
6. Don't FALL OVER your own feet.
7. We SAIL OVER the equator tomorrow.
8. WE'LL EVEN SELL EVERY stick of furniture.
9. MAIL IN your order today.
10. TELL US ALL ABOUT your vacation at dinner.
11. Let's go to the SALE ON shoes tomorrow.
12. The FEMALE LEAD has a pretty voice.

(ng) Sound

The (ng) sound is a voiced nasal sound. It is produced by raising the back of your tongue to the back part of the roof of your mouth, voicing and letting the air come out of your nose. The most common pronunciation differences are either the substitution of (in) for the (ing) word-ending, as in GOIN for GOING, or the addition of (g) after (ng) as in SINGUH for SING. Test yourself on the following words. See if you can determine which substitution you use for (ng) and if you can produce the (ng) words in SE style.

(in) - (ing)	(ng)(g) - (ng)
go in - going	ringg - ring
thin - thing	bringg - bring
some thin - something	wingg - wing
any thin - anything	flingg - fling
be in - being	strongg - strong
win in - winning	longg - long
do in - doing	banggingg - banging
sing in - singing	singgingg - singing

(ng) Words and Phrases

sing - sing a note	angry - angry at you
ring - ring the bell	coming - coming home
long - a long story	being - being happy
song - a beautiful song	seeing - seeing a movie
among - among the trees	nothing - nothing to do
along - along for the ride	something - something for her
belong - belong to us	running - running a race
thing - not a thing	selling - selling papers
longer - longer than eternity	washing - washing the car
younger - younger than I	facing - facing the music

Practice Sentences with Capitalized (ng) and (ing) Sounds

1. I am sellING my house and movING to Vermont.

2. BeING a good student means studyING and preparING.

3. WalkING in the city is interestING and invigoratING.

4. DoING somethING meanINGful for people is fulfillING.

5. PerformING on a stage is challengING and thrillING.

6. My mornING routine is bathING, brushING and dressING.

7. SingING songs while playING the piano is confusING.

8. She had riNGs on her fiNGers and baNGs on her forehead.

9. CookING, cleanING, and eatING means it's ThanksgivING.

10. He is winnING the matches by buildING up his streNGth.

11. NothING should be taken for granted; everythING counts.

12. MeanINGful looks were communicatING nonverbal feelINGs.

13. He was dribblING, passING and shootING the ball easily.

14. The kING heard the claNGING of the bell and arose.

15. The rINGING in her ears kept her from hearING the soNG.

16. LoNG, loNG ago, when we were youNG, we saNG that soNG.

17. BeING a good Boy Scout means always beING prepared.

18. BuyING a puppy means feedING, walkING and lovING it.

19. SeeING is not believING; hearING is not knowING.

20. Bells were dINGING and doNGING every Sunday evenING.

21. The youNGer you are, the aNGrier you get when losING.

22. ManagING a business means goING crazy worryING.

23. RaisING youNG children is a satisfyING experience.

24. ClearING, washING and dryING the dishes are your jobs.

Nasal Sounds: (n) or (m) - (ang) or (ing) – nasal vowels

There are three common pronunciation differences that occur with regard to the nasal sounds. The first is the substitution of (n) for (m) when the (m) occurs at the end of a word, as in CANE for CAME. The second is the substitution of (ang) for (ing), as in THANG for THING. The third difference is the production of a nasalized vowel for the final (m), (n), and (ng), as in (cã) for CAN.

Test yourself on the following word-pairs to determine which pronunciations you use for nasal consonant word-endings.

SE	DIFFERENCE	SE	DIFFERENCE
came	cane, cã	thing	thang
same	sane, sã	ring	rang
game	gain, gã	sing	sang
shame	Shane, shã	sting	stang
frame	Frain, Frã	Bing	bang
scam	scan, scã	fling	flang
jam	Jan, Jã	king	kang
time	tyne, tĩ	Bingo	bango
lime	line, lĩ	ping	pang
some	son, sõ	ding	dang

Read the following sentences in the SE style of pronunciation, making sure that you pronounce the capitalized (m), (n) and (ing) sounds.

1. I caMe to see the kING do his thING.

2. I have soMe more tiMe to play the gaMe.

3. BeN gave up everythING for a hoMe and a rING.

4. BING and ToM like jaM on bread just for fuN.

5. DaN squeezed liMe juice on his bee stING.

6. RING the doorbell agaiN to see if he's hoMe.

7. It'll be a shaMe wheN BING can't sING any more.

8. BrING me teN pING-pong paddles so I caN swING.

9. BeING aN Andy FraiN usher seeMs like a lot of fuN.

10. DaN GoldrING gave DiaNe a bell for a weddING rING.

(er) Sound

The most common difference in the pronunciation of the (er) sound is the omission of the sound when it occurs in the middle or at the end of words. It is acceptable in the eastern and southern part of the U.S. to omit (er). In the Midwest, however, where the Broadcast/General American style of English is the standard, every (er) sound in a word must be distinctly produced. Test yourself on the following word-pairs to determine if you do or do not produce (er):

OMISSION	(er)
doe	door
foe	for, four
ah	are
pay a	pair
they a	their, there
thud	third
bud	bird
gull	girl
hut	hurt
huh	her
such	search
hud	heard
bun	burn

If the first column of words above does not represent your pronunciation of each (er) word, read the second column of words again so that you hear and feel exactly the difference in pronunciation. For example, instead of DOE you may say DAW for DOOR, or, you may produce a faint "flavor" of (er) rather than a strong (er). After you have decided what it is you do instead of producing (er), read the following words with strong (er)s.

worse	third	turn	under	collar
worsen	bird	burn	over	dollar
worm	stir	purpose	mother	liar
word	dirt	purple	father	heard
worth	first	hurt	weather	search
worst	sir	Thursday	brother	earth
worthless	girl	Saturday	rather	fern

(continued)

worthy	birth	curtain	gather	her
wordy	mirth	furl	sister	nerd
wormed	dirge	curl	either	herb
fire	ear	bare	sure	for
hire	fear	dare	your	four
tire	near	fare	lure	or
wire	dear	care	poor	before
sire	clear	where	moor	store
higher	we're	air	shower	sore
choir	beer	lair	power	more
ire	sheer	stair	cower	wore
dire	deer	pair	hour	horrible
buyer	mere	fair	our	lord
car	are	tar	far	tar
card	arm	tarp	farm	start
bark	lark	march	yard	part
barn	large	market	yarn	park

Practice Sentences with Capitalized (er) Sounds

1. I feaR foR youR caR because of the geaRs and reaR axle.

2. ARe youR caRds betteR than youR motheR's caRds?

3. PaRk youR shopping caRt neaR the faRmeR's maRket.

4. We'Re weaRing theiR sweateRs and shiRts.

5. WheRe does ouR touR staRt – in PaRis oR FloRence?

6. YouR yaRd and gaRden aRe coloRful and goRgeous.

7. "EdwaRd, paRk youR caR in the HaRvaRd YaRd."

8. They'Re tiRed of climbing the staiRs to theiR laiR.

9. ORdeR fouR poRtions foR now and we'll shaRe.

10. StaRe at heR foR an houR and she'll be embaRrassed.

11. We'Re foRtunate that you'Re coming oveR to ouR place.

12. I'll iRon youR collaR foR the paRty tomoRrow.

13. We'Re writing ouR repoRt foR HistoRy.

14. ARe you going to shop foR coRn oR foR tuRnips?

15. Honk youR hoRn foR RobeRt so we'Re not taRdy.

Practice Sentences for (er) without Cues

1. The picture of the third word was under the table.
2. Her thirty-fourth birthday was Thursday.
3. Were you hurt when you fell from the horse?
4. The birds hurried to collect the worms.
5. Tell Burt to call her on the third of March.
6. Do you ever sit on the pier and watch the river?
7. The little girl stirred the water and dirt for fun.
8. Fur coats are not favorite outer garments any more.
9. The girl searched all over but her purse was gone.
10. Saturday's weather was worse than Thursday's.
11. Summer rain is always welcome.
12. The jogger raced across the finish line.
13. My mother rowed our raft to safety.
14. She took the higher road and he took the lower road.
15. The redder roses are prettier than the yellow ones.
16. Never run across a street without looking both ways.
17. My brother rode his bicycle to school every day.
18. The day seems longer and longer when you're bored.
19. I work harder and harder every year.
20. The weather will be in the forties today.

Medial (er-r) Sounds

Pronunciation differences are common when (er-r) occurs in the middle of words. One difference is the production of a "long" vowel + (r), instead of the GA/SE vowel + (er), as in PAY-RISS for P-AIR-ISS. Another difference is the omission of medial (er-r), as in PASS for PARIS. Read the following sample words and determine if you substitute (r) for medial (er-r), or omit the (er-r) medially. Read the drill words making sure that you hear and feel the GA/SE vowel + (er-r) in the middle of the words.

WORDS	DIFFERENCE	GA/SE
PARIS	pay-riss, pass	p-air-iss
CARRIED	cay-reed, cad	c-air-eed
CARROT	cay-rut, cat	c-air-ut
BORING	boh-ring, bawng	baw-er-ing
SERIOUS	see-ree-yus, sis	see-er-ee-us
PERIOD	pee-ree-yud, pid	pee-er-ee-ud

Mary	scary	parrot	fairy
married	wearing	staring	berry
Jerry	hairy	buried	daring
Gary	Larry	terrible	airy
very	sterile	apparent	shared

Practice Sentences with Capitalized Vowels + Medial (er-r) Sounds

1. LARRy and JERRy picked bERRies in FebruARy.
2. It was vERy appARent that MARy was tERRibly hAIRy.
3. GARy and SARah were mARRied in PARis on JanuARy 19th.
4. PARents are not dARing about their children mARRying.
5. He cARRied the cARRots and said it's a bORing ERRand.
6. BURying garbage is a vERy serious problem.
7. Don't tARRy or PERRy and LARRy will be vERy angry.
8. BURy the hatchet – don't cARRy a grudge.
9. StrawbERRies and bluebERRies are rare in JanuARy.
10. Be wARy of scARy, hAIRy monsters who are vERy mean.

Word-ending Consonants

We have already explained that in SE, each consonant in a consonant cluster must be pronounced. Single consonant sounds that end words also must be pronounced. The following drill presents four columns of words. Say the four words that are in each horizontal row. If they all sound the same, you are omitting the final consonants of the words in the last three columns. Say the words again, making sure that you hear and feel the production of the final consonants, and that each word ends differently.

-	d - t	b - p	k - g
Kay	Kate	cape	cake
ray	raid	rape	rake
row	wrote	robe	rogue
sow	sowed	soap	soak
tie	tight	type	tyke
see	seat	seep	seek
"A"	eight	ape	ache
Lou	lewd	lube	Luke
high	hide	hype	hike
be	bead	beep	beak
we	weed	weep	week
do	dude	dupe	duke

Practice Sentences with Capitalized Word-ending Consonant Sounds

1. Kay gaVe KaTe a caPe and caKe for her birthday.
2. LuKe gaVe Lou a high fiVe for hiS lay-uP.
3. We weeD every weeK and weeP wheN weedS grow baCK.
4. I wanT to hiDe from the hyPe abouT the hiKe.
5. I'LL cooK a steaK dinner for MiKe, NiCK and RiCK.
6. AiM at the baskeT riM wheN you shooT a free-throw.
7. The caB tooK me dowN the wroNG streeT so I goT upseT.
8. I saiD, "TaKe me to MaiN StreeT," buT he tooK me to OaK StreeT. I waS maD, so I saiD, "LeT me oFF righT here, righT now," anD he diD.

(b) and (v) Sounds

The substitution of (b) for the SE (v), as in BERRY for VERY, is a common pronunciation difference. Speakers of American Black English, and those with a foreign background like Spanish, sometimes use this substitution.

Read the following word-pairs out loud to determine how you produce (v). Do you produce it in SE style by biting down gently on your bottom lip with your top front teeth? Or, do you use two lips, resulting in the production or approximation of (b)? Practice the word-pairs until you feel and hear the difference between (b) and (v) words. Practice until the production of (v) becomes effortless.

(b)	(v)	(b)	(v)	(b)	(v)
berry	very	habit	have it	Gabe	gave
bat	vat	marble	marvel	dub	dove
best	vest	lobes	loaves	robe	rove
bowel	vowel	Gibbs	gives	curb	curve

Read the following sentences using the SE production for the capitalized (v) sounds. Note: OF is pronounced as (uhv).

1. Vincent inVited Valerie to a loVely eVening party.
2. Vinnie looked Very special in a VelVet Vest.
3. Val looked raVishing in Violet and mauVe.
4. They gaVe their gloVes and coats to the serVants.
5. They were giVen seVen kinds of appetizers and offered eleVen kinds of cold drinks.
6. They were Very braVe and tasted eVerything, even Veal.
7. They neVer had enVisioned such a Variety of Vegetables.
8. "HaVe you eVer eVen imagined something so heaVenly?" Val asked Vinnie.
9. They were diVided into new twosomes and Val loVed her new partner, GaVin.
10. Vinnie waVed to Val and moVed toward dinner with Vicky.

See page 20 for more information and drills.

(t) and (d) Sounds

These two sounds are produced identically except that (t) is voiceless, and (d) is voiced. This means that (t) is either PLODED (air is puffed out), or IMPLODED (the tongue moves up to produce it, but no air is puffed out); (d) is voiced, meaning sound is produced, not just air (see pages 20 and 47).

Two pronunciation differences commonly occur. The first difference is exaggeration of (t). GA/SE speakers often substitute a (d) sound when (t) occurs medially, and implode the (t) at the end of a word if (t) follows a vowel. Study the following word-pairs. Note the GA/SE substitution of (d) for (t) and the imploded (t) endings. Practice them until they become comfortable and effortless.

GA/SE	DIFFERENCE	GA/SE	DIFFERENCE
wriDing	wriTing	buDDer	buTTer
universiDy	universiTy	beDDer	beTTer
liDDle	liTTle	faDDer	faTTer
i(t)	iT	ge(t)	geT
a(t)	aT	le(t)	leT

The second pronunciation difference is the substitution of (t) for (d) when (d) occurs medially in a word or a phrase, followed by a consonant. Black English speakers often pronounce the medial (d) this way. Note the contrasting pronunciations below. Make sure that you feel and hear the voiced (d) when you practice.

GA/SE	BE	GA/SE	BE
haD been	haT been	riDe was	righT was
beDroom	beT room	noD for	noT for
leD him	leT him	saiD that	seT that
deaD man	debT man	NeD was	neT was
baD boy	baT boy	harDening	hearTening
faD was	faT was	birD had	BerT had

Practice Sentences with Cued (t) and (d) Sounds

1. ThaD was tha(t) liDDle baD boy who maDe tha(t) kiD maD.

2. UniversiDy graD students a(t) HarvarD College ge(t) jobs.

3. She's maD tha(t) NeD diD no(t) have gooD grades, bu(t) go(t) gooD jobs a(t) all the "righ(t)" companies.

(continued)

4. She wro(t)e a leDDer to PeDer bu(t) diD he answer i(t)?

5. LyDia leD him to the deaD man who'D been burieD for days.

6. The preDDy birD haD landeD righ(t) on her heaD band.

7. The more buDDer you ea(t), the faDDer you ge(t). Righ(t)?

8. BeDDer ge(t) to work righ(t) away or you'll be la(t)e.

9. DaD go(t) a lo(t) of leDDers tha(t) saiD, "Call laDer."

10. She saDly tolD him tha(t) he was no(t) the one for her.

11. The riDe was bumpy anD maDe her sick.

12. She turneD on the ligh(t).

(j) and (y) Sounds

If you have a foreign-language background, you may use different pronunciations for the English (j) and (y). You may substitute (j) as in JELLO for (y) as in YELLOW and vice versa. The SE (j) is produced by raising both the tip and middle part of your tongue to the roof of your mouth (hard palate) and making a sound that is voiced and explosive, not sustained. The (y) is produced by raising only the middle of the tongue to the hard palate, and making a sound that is voiced and sustained – similar to the Spanish (LL) as in LLAMA and (y) as in YO. When "y" ends a word or comes after a vowel, it becomes a vowel, like (ee) in PARTY and (ay) in PLAY.

Practice the following word-pairs, making sure that you feel and hear the English sounds. Note that the English (j) sound is sometimes spelled with "g."

(j)	(y)	(j)	(y)	(j)	(y)
Jack	yak	Jay	yea!	major	mayor
gyp	yip	jail	Yale	danger	Dan, your
jam	yam	jeer	year	ranger	rain your
Jew	you	jewel	you'll	stranger	strain your
Jello	yellow	Jess	yes	waging	weighing
jet	yet	jot	yacht	gauger	gayer
juice	use	joke	yolk	Granger	gray your
gel	yell	John	yon	manger	main your

Practice the following sentences with capitalized (j) and (y) sounds. Note that (y) has various vowel-spellings, like "io" and "u."

1. Jess said, "Yes!" when Jay's club asked him to Join.
2. You'll be in no danGer if the ranGer is Your friend.
3. If You fly in a Jet, You'll have to Yell to be heard.
4. John Joked that the maYor likes Yachting, not Jetting.
5. The Juice was not Yet poured, the Jam was not Yet spread, and the Jello was not Yet Jelled.
6. Jesse James is a leGendary figUre like John DillinGer.
7. Do You eat onIOns with the Yolk of Your fried egg?
8. The Los AnGeles DoDGers Used to play in Brooklyn, N.Y., but the New York Yankees are still there.

(ch) and (sh) Sounds

If you have a foreign-language background, you might need to learn the production of the English (sh) and/or (ch). Spanish-speakers, for instance, often substitute (ch) for (sh), as in CHIP for SHIP, because they do not have (sh) in their phonetic system.

The English (sh) is voiceless and SUSTAINED. It is produced by raising the middle of your tongue to the hard palate, and "pooching" your lips while you exhale a stream of air. The English (ch) is produced in the same manner as the (sh), but it is an EXPLOSIVE puff of air. (See page 20 for more drills.)

Practice the following word-pairs. Make sure that you feel and hear the sustained duration of (sh) and the explosive duration of (ch). Note: TION words are pronounced as SHUN with an (sh); CHICAGO, MACHINE, and CHEVROLET, although spelled with (ch), are pronounced with (sh) sounds.

(sh)	(ch)	(sh)	(ch)	(sh)	(ch)
ship	chip	washing	watching	wash	watch
sheet	cheat	cashing	catching	cash	catch
shore	chore	mashing	matching	mash	match
share	chair	lashing	latching	lash	latch
she's	cheese	marshes	marches	marsh	march
sheep	cheap	crushes	crutches	mush	much
shoe	chew	dishes	ditches	wish	witch
sheer	cheer	mashed	matched	dish	ditch
Sherry	cherry	hashed	hatched	bush	Butch
sheaf	chief	washer	watcher	bash	batch

Practice Sentences with Capitalized (sh) Sounds

1. SHerry's SHeets SHrank in the waSHing maCHine.

2. SHe wiSHes for more caSH maCHines in CHicago staTIOns.

3. The SHipping staTIOn cruSHed her SHiny CHevrolet sedan.

4. The SHip-to-SHore maCHine was calling CHicago.

5. SHe waSHed the diSHes and he maSHed the muSHy potatoes.

6. SHe watched her unleaSHed dog cruSH her rose buSHes.

7. The gaSH in her cherry wood furniture ruined her cheerful nature and disposiTIOn.

8. The creaTIOn and compleTIOn of art brings satisfacTIOn.

(v) and (w) Sounds

If English is not your primary language, you might substitute (w) for (v), as in WARY for VARY, and vice versa. Even if you know how to produce both sounds, you may need to practice getting used to the English pronunciation of the letters. When you see "v," bite down gently on your lower lip and voice a sustained sound; when you see "w," put your slightly-rounded lips together and voice it. (See page 20 for more exercises on voiced sounds.)

Practice the following word-pairs. Note that in English, "w" is sometimes a silent vowel.

(w)	(v)		(w)	(v)		SILENT	(v)
went	vent		rowing	roving		rowed	roved
wary	vary		rower	rover		grow	grove
we'll	veal		mooing	moving		stow	stove
we're	veer		grower	Grover		grew	groove

Read the following sentences. The "v" and "w" letters are capitalized when the corresponding SE pronunciation is necessary. Note that OF is pronounced (uhv).

1. DeVelop your Voice and you Will be on teleVision.
2. The grape groWers oF Burgundy sell a Variety oF Wines.
3. SteVen deserVes a reWard for renoVating his liVingroom.
4. Linda LaVin Was Very funny as Alice on teleVision.
5. We should loVe oUr enVironment as Well as oUrselVes.
6. LaVinia Wishes that One oF you Would giVe her a new Wallet before she goes aWay on Vacation.
7. The SeVen-EleVen on Western AVenue sells moVie reViews.
8. OliVia saVed seVenty cents for William and Vice Versa.
9. DaVid Went With HoWard to Watch the moVers moVe all the furniture into the moVing Van.
10. We alWays haVe Wonderful eVenings at RaVinia FestiVal.
11. IrVing Will inVite LaVelle to preView the moVie.
12. On the last Wednesday oF NoVember, We alWays haVe fun chopping Vegetables and Wiping dishes for ThanksgiVing.

(p) and (f) Sounds

If English is not your primary language, you might substitute the (p) sound for the (f) sound, as in PIG for FIG. The (p) is a VOICELESS sound that you produce by puffing out an explosion of air with your two lips. The (f) is also a VOICELESS sound that is produced by biting gently on your bottom lip with your top front teeth and hissing out a sustained stream of air. (See page 20 for more exercises and information on Voiced and Voiceless consonants.)

Practice the following word-pairs. Note that the letter combinations of "ph," as in PHONE, and sometimes "gh," as in LAUGH, are pronounced as (f) sounds.

(p)	(f)	(p)	(f)	(p)	(f)
pit	fit	snipping	sniffing	cup	cuff
pad	fad	supper	suffer	wipe	wife
paint	faint	puppy	puffy	clip	cliff
pool	fool	loped	loafed	leap	leaf
pail	fail	laps	laughs	cheap	chief
pill	Phil	tips	tiffs	hoop	hoof
pone	phone	reaps	reefs	lap	laugh
past	fast	sipped	sift	lope	loaf
peel	feel	snipped	sniffed	sheep	sheaf
pun	fun	tips	tiffs	pup	puff

Read the following sentences. Make sure that you feel and hear the (f) sound in words that contain the capitalized letters.

1. Frank and Frances reFrain From eating Fatty Foods.

2. Fix PHil, some beeF, French Fries and coFFee.

3. My Favorite giFt is a beautiFul array of Flowers.

4. Do you Feel like having breakFast at a wonderFul caFe?

5. My Father and his Friends play golF every Friday.

6. My Friend telePHoned to see iF we Felt like a Fish-Fry.

7. I lauGHed when Five elePHants liFted their Front Feet.

8. Fred brings me coFFee to the oFFice at Four on Friday.

9. Franny Feeds her Fish From a Fork until they are Full!

10. My Favorite PHotograPHs are of snowFlakes, butterFlies, and beautiFul, digniFied giraFFes.

11. Running bare-Footed in Farm Fields Felt Funny but Fine.

12. Penny petted the playFul, soFt and beautiFul puppy.

13. The toFFee that was oFFered For Free made me couGH.

14. LiFting pounds of Frozen Foods was Fatiguing.

15. TelePHoning Friends is what Fourteen year-olds Favor.

16. PHyllis and PHil lauGHed and lauGHed until they Fell.

17. YusuF preFers Ferociously caFFeinated coFFee with spoonFuls of Foamy HalF & HalF.

18. CaFeteria Food Fails to satisFy StePHanie For breakFast.

19. Felicia is FiFty-Four; RalPH is FiFty-Five; and their Four oFFspring, Frank, FiFi, PHil and MuFFy are FiFteen, Fourteen, Five and Four.

20. I Feel that a party For a Few Friends is more Fun than one For Forty or Fifty Friends.

21. It's Fun to visit CaliFornia or Florida in February.

22. PHyllis and Frank are good Friends who live in PHiladelPHia.

23. Little Felix leFt his Favorite, soFt, stuFFed animal in his First grade classroom at Frederick Douglass School.

24. It's diFFicult to Find the perFect platForm shoes to Fit your Feet.

25. The Fancy French restaurant serves Five diFFerent types of Fish, ButterFly Shrimp, Filet Mignon and French Fries.

Chapter 3: Vowel Sounds

Vowel Sounds + (L)

There are several instances when the production of vowel sounds differs from the Broadcast/Standard English style of pronunciation. A common difference occurs when (L) follows a vowel. (See also page 36.)

(ihl) - (eel) Contrast

The first vowel-production contrast is between (ih) as in IT and (ee) as in HE, when they occur before (L). The most common difference from GA/SE pronunciation is the reversal of the two vowels, as in HILL for HEEL and vice versa. If this is what you hear and feel after reading the following word-pairs, read them again, making sure that when you read the (eel) words, you feel yourself smiling as you produce (ee); when you read (ih), your lips will feel neutral.

(ihl)	(eel)	
hill	heal, he'll	(he ill)
shill	she'll	(she ill)
will	we'll	(we ill)
pill	peel, peal	(pee ill)
rill	reel, real	(ree ill)
fill	feel	(fee ill)
dill	deal	(dee ill)
mill	meal	(me ill)
sill	seal	(see ill)
a pill	appeal	a (pee ill)
still	steal, steel	(stee ill)
ill	eel	(ee ill)
kill	keel	(key ill)
nil	kneel, Neil	(knee ill)

Practice Sentences with Capitalized (ihl)-(eel) Sounds

1. HE'LL fEEL ILL, take a pILL, but not eat the mEAL.

2. SEALs rEALly appEAL to the EELs in ILLinois.

3. NEIL wILL not stEAL the whEELs from ShEILa's car.

4. ShE'LL stILL fEEL ILL but BILL wILL go without her.

5. We fEEL that ILLinois has rEAL good dEALs for mEALs.

(ehl) - (ayl) Contrast

GA/SE speakers pronounce the "e" in the following (L) words like the (eh) in BET; the "a" before (L) sounds like the (ay) in DATE. If you are from the south or southwest, you might substitute (ah-ee) for (ay). The other common pronunciation difference is reversing the vowels and saying MALE for MEL and MEL for MALE. Read the following word-pairs. Make sure that you feel your lips smile for the (ayl) words and stay more neutral for the (ehl) words.

(ehl)	(ayl)	
Mel	male, mail	(may ill)
fell	fail	(Fay ill)
el	ale, ail	(A ill)
bell	bale, bail	(bay ill)
dell	dale	(day ill)
hell	hale, hail	(hay ill)
gel	jail	(Jay ill)
Nell	nail	(nay ill)
quell	quail	(quay ill)
sell	sail	(say ill)
tell	tale, tail	(tay ill)
well	wail	(way ill)
excel	exhale	(hay ill)
yell	Yale	(yay ill)

Practice Sentences with Capitalized (ehl) and (ayl) Sounds

1. MEL is a mALe who goes to YALe and sAILs.

2. NELL is a femALe who excELs at sELLing nAILs.

3. When MEL fELL in the pAIL, NELL started to wAIL.

4. MEL yELLs at NELL when she fAILs to bAIL him out of jAIL and when she tELLs him to sELL his sAILboat.

(continued)

5. TELL a tALe wELL, and mALes and femALes from YALe will hAIL you as an excELLent tALe-tELLer who excELs at exhALing and inhALing wELL when tELLing tALes.

6. The bELL on the EL fAILed to ring when it stopped at ELm Street.

7. The Farmer in the DELL had to sELL his quAILs.

8. The mALe whALe flipped his tAIL.

(ile) - (owl) Contrast

The third vowel-production contrast is the substitution of (owl) for (ile), as in FOWL for FILE. This difference is complicated if you also omit (L) from a consonant cluster and/or from the final position of a word as in CHOWED for CHILD and POW for PILE (see pages 8, 36 and 61).

Read the following word-pairs and determine whether you say (owl) for (ile) and/or omit (L). Read them again, making sure that you hear yourself saying (ah-ee) + (L) + the consonant, when there is one.

(ow) + (L)	i (ah-ee) + (L)
fowl or fow	file
Powell or pow	pile
towel or tow	tile
bowel or bow	bile
dowel or Dow	dial
owl or ow	isle, aisle
vowel or vow	vile
chow or chowed	child
pow or powed	piled

Practice Sentences with Capitalized i (ah-ee) + (L) Sounds

1. The chILd smILed as she made a pILe of the blocks.

2. WhILe I fILed the papers, he dIALed the numbers.

3. The IsLe of Hawaii has mILes and mILes of sand.

4. Don't rILe Mrs. NILes or she'll pILe on the homework.

5. We fILed down the AIsLe in mannerly stYLe.

6. She begUILed him with her smILe.

7. I'LL fILe the papers whILe you put them in pILes.

8. The chILd's denIAL was ignored because of his smILe.

9. The trIAL was held mILes from where the crime occurred.

10. I'LL help you with the tILes if you don't get rILed.

(ahl) - (awl) Contrast

The fourth difference in vowel-production occurs when (ah) is substituted for (aw) before (L). Read the following word-pairs. When you read the words in the (ahl) column, open your mouth and pretend you are saying "ah" for the doctor. Remember to "pooch" your lips for the (aw) or it will sound like (ah). Remember to produce final (L)s.

(ahl)	(awl)	MORE (aw) WORDS
collar	call	stall
follow	fall	Paul
Polly	Paul	pall
Molly	mall	maul
dollar	Rudolph	shawl
golly	gall	drawl
holly	haul	hall
Ollie	all	crawl
wallow	wall	tall

Practice Sentences with the (awl) Sounds Capitalized

1. In the fALL, we ALL play bALL and watch leaves fALL.

2. PAUL's car stALLed and we were ALL late to Molly's.

3. The wALLs in the hALL ALL had family photos on them.

4. ALL of Polly's dolls had collars and shAWLs on.

5. The baby crAWLed through the hALL ALL the way to me.

6. FALL on the bALL, but don't mAUL PAUL or he'll cALL ALL of his tALL bALL-playing friends.

7. In basebALL, foul bALLs cause many fALLs.

(continued)

8. In footbALL, tALL tacklers stALL progress.

9. In basketbALL, even though you're not tALL, you can stALL by dribbling the bALL cleverly.

10. RudOLph and PAUL painted ALL the wALLs in the hALL.

11. A Southerner's drAWL is ALways pleasing to the ear.

12. If you fumble the bALL, ALways fALL on it.

Practice Sentences for (L): in CONSONANT CLUSTERS, in the FINAL POSITION OF WORDS, and AFTER CONTRASTING VOWELS

1. Hold the cold jello mold while I fill it up to full.

2. He hailed himself ruler, but his title was "Fool."

3. The golden bell knolled the time for the hill people.

4. They almost killed themselves pole vaulting.

5. I bailed him out of jail, then tailed him myself.

6. Althea wailed because she almost failed the oral exam.

7. Wolves are valuable animals and Walter helped them.

8. Although it wasn't my fault, I felt guilty.

9. I told my uncle that I had sold the gold already.

10. I dialed Paul's number but Jill answered.

11. Fill all the shelves with food for homeless people.

12. He told us that he had sailed around the world.

13. The baby's skin felt almost like velvet.

14. You will have control if you feel that you do.

15. The old woman hauled the pile of coal up the hill.

16. She fell, and rolled and rolled back down the hill.

17. He should help himself and we should help ourselves.

18. We'll help him hold the nails while he hammers.

19. Mel called to his pals who chased balls in the field.

20. The el rumbled and squealed but failed to stop.

21. Althea almost always folded the piles of unsealed mail.

22. Tell me an old tale and then I'll tell you one.

(ih) and (eh) + (m), (n), (ng) Sounds

When GA/SE speakers pronounce the words below, the "i" sounds like (ih) as in BIT, using relaxed lips; the "e" sounds like (eh), as in BET, using half-smiling lips. The most common pronunciation differences occur when PIN and PEN both sound like PIN, or when the vowels are reversed, so that PIN sounds like PEN and vice versa. Practice the word-pairs, making sure that your lips are half-smiling for (eh). Please note that ANY and MANY are (eh) words, and BEEN is an (ih) word.

(ih) + (n)-(m)-(ng)	(eh) + (n)-(m)-(ng)
pin	pen
finger	Fenger
din	den
lint	Lent
mint	meant
inny	any
in	En
quint	Quent
sinned	send
win	when
Lynn	Len
kin	Ken
inter-	enter
him	hem
Minny	many
since	cents
bin, been	Ben
Wynn's day	Wednesday

Practice Sentences with Capitalized (ih) and (eh) + (n), (m), (ng) Sounds

1. I sENt hIM a note that I pENNed IN a blue tINt.

2. LYNN remEMbered that the pIN had a splENdid gEM IN it.

3. JIM ENtertained LEN and KEN IN the cENtral dEN.

4. BENjamIN met tEN friENds from MEMphis, TENNessee.

5. GINNy's hEM needed to be pINNed and pressed.

(continued)

6. BEN hadn't bEeN to ANy friENd's sINce WEdNesday.

7. MINNy sENt JENNy mANy memENtos from PENNsylvania.

8. DENNis wENt to lENd LYNn a tENt-mENdING kit.

Now continue without cues.

9. The din from the laughing men made Quenton grin.

10. It's lamentable that she sent them to Denver.

11. The temperature is in the low twenties.

12. You'll win when you sense weakness in your enemy.

13. Don't lend any money to friends.

14. She sinned when she spent all her friend's money.

15. Linda Benjamin and Ginny Jensen went to South Bend.

16. Let's pretend that Barbie and Ken went away forever.

17. Tomorrow's temperature in Indiana will be ten below.

18. The rental fee for the tent made Lenny angry.

19. Jim sent his girlfriend a sensational engagement gem.

20. She sent him a tinny pin from a five and ten cent shop.

21. Then she went and had an expensive coin minted for him.

22. Raise ten fingers if you went to Fenger High School.

23. The stench from the garbage made Len and Lynn wince.

24. In November and December, the temperature descends.

25. Jim's dimples entertain his many feminine friends.

26. Ken sent Jennifer rings and things of genuine expense.

27. Lynn intended to entice him with feminine endeavors.

28. The advertisement meant to encourage spending.

29. Men in a democratic society have to contend with women.

30. The French never intend to send tentative messages.

Pure Vowel – Diphthong Contrasts:
(ah) - (ah-ee)   (aw) - (aw-ee)   (ah) - (ah-oh)

It is standard pronunciation in the southern states to substitute one pure vowel sound for a diphthong (a two-vowel sound). For example, if you say TOM for TIME, BAW or BO for BOY, and/or HAH for HOW, you are producing one vowel, rather than the General American two-vowel glide.

Say the following words to determine which vowels you are using. Note the phonetic spellings of the diphthongs. Practice them, making sure that your lips smile for the (ee) endings and are rounded for the (oh) endings.

(ah)	(ah-ee)	(aw)	(aw-ee)	(ah)	(ah-oh)
ah	I, eye	aw	"oy"	Ah	ow
Tom	time	tall	toil	"tahl"	towel
sot	sight	sore	Sawyer	tsar	sour
not	night	"naws"	noise	"nah"	now
hot	height	haw	Hoy	hah	how
plot	plight	"plaw"	ploy	"plah"	plow
rot	right	raw	Roy	rah	Rau
cot	kite	caw	coy	"cah"	cow
lock	like	laud	Lloyd	"lahd"	loud
bah!	by, bye	"bawed"	Boyd	"bod"	bowed
fond	find	"fawed"	foil	"fahl"	foul

Practice Sentences with Two-Vowel Diphthongs Capitalized

1. I fInd that I'm fond of rIding mY bIke at nIght.
2. Tom SAWyer lIked the cOY plOY of whIte-washing.
3. ROY and I made nOIse tOIling lOUdly with the plOW.
4. I'll lIE on my sIde watching the fIre on FrIday nIghts.
5. I trIEd to fInd the fIve mIce in mY prIcey tOWnhOUse.
6. I lIke Irish stew, HawAIian pIneapples, and ThAI rIce.
7. LlOYd and RAU fOUnd OUt that JOY lIked both bOYs.
8. HOY was lOYal to the ROYals, not the DetrOIt TIgers.
9. I fOUnd OUt that ROY's vOIce sOUnded nOIsy and lOUd.
10. The sOIled tOWel was DOYle's, not SImon's or mIne.

(ah) - (aw) Contrast

This lesson explains when GA/SE speakers use (ah) and (aw), and how each is pronounced. The (ah) is produced with an open jaw – the same sound you produce when the doctor asks you to "say ah." The (aw) sound is produced with rounded lips as well as an open jaw (see page 61). The most common pronunciation difference is the substitution of (ah) for (aw) as in COT for CAUGHT, and sometimes, vice versa. Read the following word-pairs and determine which substitution you use. Make sure you round your lips for the (aw) words. Note that ON is an (ah) word.

(ah)	(aw)	MORE (aw) WORDS
on	–	–
upon	a pawn	fall
Lon	lawn	call
fond	fawned	ball
pond	pawned	brought
cod	cawed	moss
pod	pawed	fought
sod	sawed	lost
hock	hawk	wash
chock	chalk	adorable
tock	talk	court
cot	caught	north
yon	yawn	wall

Practice Sentences with Capitalized (aw) Sounds

1. I was stAlled by fAlling over the tAll wAll.

2. The dOg cAUGHt the bAll, then pAWed the sod fOr mOre.

3. The crow cAWed at the hAWk, then fOUGHt fOr lOng worms.

4. I sAW lots of lAWn mowers crAWling alOng the lAWns.

5. All the adOrable tots were yAWning while on the cots.

6. I bOUGHt three wOks and two fOrks at the mAll.

7. DAWn brOUGHt fOUr fAWns fOr us to wAtch in AUgust.

8. LAUra lOst the fOUr adOrable hOgs that PAUl bOUght.

(ih) - (ee) Contrast

If you speak Southern SE, American BE, or you have a foreign-language background, your pronunciation of these vowels may differ from GA/SE. The most common differences for American-born speakers are: substitution of (ee) as in DEED, for (ih) as in DID, and vice versa; substitution of (ih) for (ee), as in (par-tih) for PARTY (par-tee). Foreign-language background speakers also reverse the two vowels so that DID becomes DEED and vice versa.

Practice the following word-pairs. Make sure that your lips are neutral for (ih); your lips smile for (ee). Do NOT glide into an (uh) after the (ee).

(ih)	(ee)	(ih)	(ee)	(ih)	(ee)
hit	heat	did	deed	bit	beat
it	eat	it's	eats	fit	feet
sit	seat	his	he's	ship	sheep
mill	meal	fill	feel	tin	teen
slip	sleep	rip	reap	mitt	meet

Practice the following sentences which have the (ih) and (ee) capitalized.
Remember: the word-ending "y" is pronounced as an (ee).

1. HE's sure that It's hIs sEAt that hE's sIttIng In.
2. HE dId a good dEEd wIth EAse and hE's fEEling proud.
3. ThIs mEAl wIll fIll us up and wE'll fEEl stuffed.
4. ThEse prEttY shoes don't fIt JEAn's tinY fEEt.
5. ThIs tEEny tInny shIp fIlls Its hold wIth shEEp.
6. HE's hIs lIttle sIster's sItter when shE's aslEEp.
7. MEEt MIster MIlls who manufactures baseball mItts.
8. ThIs chIcken dInner costs the lEAst on the menu's lIst.
9. HIs kIn want to mEEt the preppy tEEns that lIve EAst.
10. ShE'll mIss TIm terribly when hE lEAves for IndIana.
11. "It's not EAsy bEIng grEEn," Is a popular fEElIng.
12. EAt thIs bIt of chEEse to fIll you untIl dInner.

The "Chicago A," and the (eh)-(a) Contrast

The vowel sound (a), as in BAT, is produced with a widely opened jaw and slightly smiling lips. One common pronunciation difference is that the speaker nasalizes and produces two vowels (diphthongizes), resulting in BEE-YAT. Some Midwesterners, particularly Chicagoans, will recognize that difference as a feature of their pronunciation style. Another difference is the reversal of (eh) and (a) so that HAD is pronounced like HEAD and vice versa (see page 65).

Practice the following (a) words making sure that:

1. Your jaw is opened widely.

2. Your lips are in a SLIGHT, not wide SMILE.

3. You do NOT feel air coming out of your nose.

4. Your tongue is relaxed and low in your mouth.

5. You hear and feel only ONE VOWEL sound.

bat	and	sad	sang	pass	fast
hat	sand	bad	rang	gas	last
fat	land	dad	have	grass	past
sat	band	had	half	mass	nasty
that	stand	mad	laugh	class	master
man	dance	can	can't	after	has

Practice Sentences with Capitalized (a) Sounds

1. DAn's clAss hAs a lAb And he cAn't stAnd thAt.

2. GrAb the bAt, stAnd At the plate, And smAsh thAt ball.

3. LAst SAturday, NAncy And StAnley hAd a snAck At a cAfe.

4. The fAt Animal hAd everyone lAUghing At its Antics.

5. After the brAt was nAsty he was too fAst to cAtch.

6. HAlf pAst nine is a fAncy-sounding time for the dAnce.

7. HAve you hAd thAt bAnd At your clAss dAnces?

8. HAs the mAn thAnked you for hAving his glAsses ready?

9. StAnd At attention or Accept the MAster Sargeant's anger.

10. Answer the mAth problem or you'll not pAss the exAm.

11. FAsten seat belts so Accidents won't be cAtastrophic.

12. DAn found rAts As big As cAts in SAm's CAfe.

(a), (ih), (eh) and (ay) Contrasts

Other pronunciation differences occur with regard to the (a) sound. The following word lists represent vowels that are often substituted for (a). Before you practice the words, review the description on page 64 of how to produce (a). Then, practice the individual vowel productions, using the following descriptions as your guide:

(ih): neutral lips, not diphthongized: pages 59 and 63.

(eh): slightly smiling lips, not diphthongized: pages 63 and 64.

(ay): smiling lips, diphthongizing (gliding) from (ay) to (ee).

(a)	(ih)	(eh)	(ay)
bad	bid	bed	bade
pan	pin	pen	pain
fan	fin	fen	feign
mass	miss	mess	mace
last	list	lest	laced
sat	sit	set	sate
pat	pit	pet	pate
gnat	knit	net	Nate
batter	bitter	better	baiter
tack	tick	tech	take

The following sentences are not cued. Read them so that you produce the GA/SE vowels as described above.

1. The last batter hit badly and sat down.
2. The clock ticks while Miss Kim sits and knits.
3. Ken better not mess the bed lest the pet get a yelling.
4. Wade feigned a pain and waited for his cane.
5. It's not better to be bitter about the batter falling.
6. Knit the net so Nate can catch the gnat.
7. Pat the pet on the pate because he fell in the pit.
8. Don't take the tools that ticky-tacky technology made.
9. Ted and Ned led the rest of the pets into the bedroom.
10. Bade him to bid on the bad bed.

Unstressed (uh): the "Schwa"

Many native-born Americans and foreign-born English speakers find the SCHWA a difficult sound to produce. The schwa is an unstressed (uh). It is produced by opening the jaw slightly, keeping the tongue relaxed and the lips unrounded. Its characteristic is neutrality.

The schwa is disguised by several different vowel-spellings. For example, the letters in the following words that are NOT CAPITALIZED represent the SE schwa, or unstressed (uh).

aDORaBLE   QUIeT   oFFICiaL   DISaPPOINTED   CIRCuS

If you are American-born, your particular English dialect may STRESS the FIRST SYLLABLES of words for which SE uses the schwa. Many speakers of BE, and other English dialects, pronounce the first and third words as:

AY-dor-uh-ble   OH-fish-uhl

If you have a Spanish-speaking background, you might pronounce the first four words with Spanish vowel-sounds.

AH-dor-AH-ble   qui-AYt   OH-fish-ee-AHL   dis-AH-pointed

The GA/SE pronunciation of the schwa-syllables is as follows. The stressed syllables are capitalized.

uh-DOR-uh-ble   QUI-uht   uh-FISH-uhl   dis-uh-POIN-ted

Study the contrasting pronunciations of the following words to determine how you produce the vowels that should be schwas. If you sometimes, or always, use a pronunciation that differs from the unstressed (uh), practice the words until (uh) becomes comfortable and UNEXAGGERATED.

WORDS	GA/SE SCHWA	DIFFERENCE
idea	i-DEE-uh	i-dee-AH
uniform	YOU-nuh-form	you-NEE-form
president	PREZ-uh-dent	pre-ZEE-dent
disapprove	dis-uh-PROVE	dis-AY-prove, dis-AH-prove

WORDS	GA/SE SCHWA	DIFFERENCE
police	puh-LEES	POH-lees
Detroit	duh-TROIT	DEE-troit
above	uh-BUHV	AY-buhv, AH-bove
addition	uh-DIH-shuhn	AY-dih-shun, AH-dee-she-OHN
opinion	uh-PIN-yuhn	OH-pin-yun, OH-PEEN-yohn
disappear	dis-uh-PEER	dis-AY-peer, dees-AH-peer

Read the following words, using the unstressed (uh) when a vowel is NOT CAPITALIZED. Remember that the schwa is neutral and should not be exaggerated. Use the visual cue of the lowercase letters to remind you of the unstressed nature of the schwa.

aPPOINTMeNT	ECHeLON	uPON	NOTiCEaBLE
DISaBILiTY	AToM	aTOMIC	DeLICiouS
REaLIZE	MENaCE	SALaD	oFFICIATE
PoLITE	aRRANGE	aPPEAR	uNTIL
PoSITioN	INVITATioN	NATioN	ReLATioN
CaTASTRoPHE	PHILOSoPHY	DiRECT	DeTERMiNE
DeSIGN	DeTROIT	PoLICE	SuGGEST
SuCCESS	DeLINEATE	DeBATE	DiVISioN
DiVINE	aLONG	aPART	aMONG
aGAINST	aSSORTED	aMID	aRISE
a MAN	a JOB	a DESK	a WOMaN
CALiFORNia	CHiCAGO	BOSToN	DaKOTa

Read the following sentences, using the unstressed (uh) when it appears as a lowercase letter in a capitalized word. Remember: always use the schwa for the word, A, and for THE when it precedes a word that begins with a consonant.

1. It's DISaPPOINTING that FINANCiaL SuCCESS DoeS not always bring EMOTioNaL GRATiFiCATioN.

2. THe DeSIGN oF a building DeTERMINES WHaT its aPPEARaNCE and FUNCTioN will be.

(continued)

3. We DeBATED aMONG ourselves and DeCIDED to call THe PoLICE DePARTMeNT and ask for an oFFICiaL DeTECTIVE.

4. The aDORaBLE school CHILDReN needed a desk, a set oF SCIeNCE books, and PENCiLS for THe classroom.

5. She REaLIZED that THe PRoDuCTioN oF aTOMIC WEAPoNRY WaS BECoMING a SERIouS PROBLeM.

6. aCQUIRING a new DIaLECT is a DIFFiCuLT job.

7. a PERSoN with a PHYSiCaL DISaBILiTY faces a lot oF DISaPPOINTMENTS, PREJuDICE and FRuSTRATioN.

8. SoLIDIFY your thoughts before you face your oPPONENT in a DeBATE or an INFORMaL DISCUSSioN.

9. COMPeTITioN is THe key to AMERiCaN CAPITaLISM.

10. THe PoLITiCaL process is THe key to AMERiCaN DeMOCRaCY.

11. The aMERiCaN eLECTioNS are PRECEDeD by a long and EXPENSiVE campaign.

12. THe PoLICE OFFiCER aRRESTeD THe WOMaN who had STOLeN THe BRACELeT from THe DiSPLAY counter.

13. SALESPERSoNS EXPERIeNCE a lot oF REJECTioN.

14. COLLeGE GRADUaTES have a better chance oF CoMPETING in THe job MARKeT than those PERSoNS who do not have a COLLeGE DiPLOMa.

15. Are you aWARE oF THe fact that you don't have eNOUGH UNiFORMS for your WAITReSSeS?

16. We had to call an AMBULaNCE for a CUSToMER at one oF THe RESTauRANTS in DeTROIT because he got ill from THe SALaD.

17. It was DISaPPOINTING to aMANDa that her COMPaNY'S PoLITE and oFFICiaL hiring an PRoMOTING POLiCIES were DIFFEReNT from THe ACTUal PRACTiCeS.

18. THe DeSIGN oF THE aPARTMeNT building and THe PoSITioNING oF its CeMENT SuPPORTS were DiRECTLY ReSPONSiBLE for THe CoLLAPSE oF THe roof.

19. THe FORMal aFFAIR to which I was INVITeD turned out to be a DISaPPOINTING CaTASTRoPHE, but THe dinner was DeLICiouS.

20. HUMaN beings' aCHIEVEMeNTS should be judged by how much they give back to SoCIeTY, not how much money or MaTERIaL they take out oF it.

Stressed (uh) - (o͝o) Contrast

The schwa, or unstressed (uh), was presented on page 66. The stressed (uh) is exactly the same sound as the schwa, but it occurs in syllables that are accented, often in one-syllable words. For example, the following one-syllable words are all pronounced with a stressed (uh).

but	come	does	drug	Cubs	buck	one	buzzer	love
rut	some	must	stun	rubs	luck	sun	drugs	done

If you are an American Southern and/or BE speaker, you might use the (o͝o) as in BOOK instead of the stressed (uh), so that CUBS sounds like C(o͝o)BS rather than the GA/SE C(UH)BS. **Practice the following word-pairs, making sure that the stressed (uh) is produced with neutral lips, not the rounded lips that we use for (o͝o).**

(uh)	(o͝o)	Practice Sentences
luck	look	LOOK and you'll find GOOD LUCK pennies.
tuck	took	She TOOK a TUCK in his pants.
huff	hoof	The horse will HUFF and stamp his HOOF.
putt	put	She PUT the PUTT right in the CUP.
cud	could	The cow COULD chew his CUD.
buck	book	It cost ONE BUCK for the BOOK.
Huck	hook	HUCK TOOK the HOOK for his raft.
stud	stood	The STUD stallion STOOD alone.

Many Southern and/or BE speakers use the stressed (uh) instead of the GA/SE medial (er). **Try the following drill:**

(uh)	(er)	Practice Sentences
bud	bird	The BIRD landed on the flower BUD.
Hud	heard	I HEARD HUD was visiting our street.
gull	girl	The GIRL watched the GULL on the beach.
hull	hurl	HURL the rock toward the boat's HULL.
huh?	her	HUH? Tell HER to speak more loudly.

Practice Sentences with Capitalized Stressed (uh) Sounds

1. DOES HUCK LOVE HONEY or the OTHER girl, SUNNY?

2. ONCE you take DRUGS FROM BUDDIES, you have TROUBLE.

3. SOME OF the MOTHERS and fathers LOVE the CUBS.

4. He WAS LUCKY that the PUCK did not CUT his THUMB.

5. He PUMPED iron on MONDAYS and SUNDAYS to build MUSCLES.

6. HUGGING PUPPIES and chewing GUM is FUN for SOME OF US.

7. RUN the OTHER way so that my COUSIN DOESN'T find US.

8. SUN and FUN are worth the MONEY.

9. SOMEONE is COMING in our FRONT door.

10. COME and STUDY at ONE o'clock on SUNDAY.

11. FROM MONDAY to SUNDAY, JUSTIN LOVES to RUN UNDER the SUN.

12. DOUG MUST quit smoking so his LUNGS BECOME clean.

13. SUNNY'S HUSBAND LOVES to HUNT for old RUGS.

14. PUNTERS LOVE to PUNT the ball to the ONE yard line.

15. EVERYONE in BUDDY'S family MUST HUG each OTHER on SUNDAYS.

16. SOMEONE is making FUN OF RUSTY'S PUG-nosed dog.

17. Bear CUBS LOVE to RUB UP against trees and eat HONEY.

18. DOES your SON like to STUDY on SUNDAYS or MONDAYS?

19. It's FUN to have COMPANY COME over for SUPPER ONCE a MONTH.

20. SOMETIMES, having nothing to do is FUN and COMFORTING.

(o͝o) - (u) Contrast

If you have a foreign-language background, you might substitute (u) as in POOL for (o͝o) as in PULL and vice versa. Practice the following word drill and sentences, making sure that your LIPS are VERY ROUNDED and TENSED for (u) and SLIGHTLY ROUNDED and RELAXED for (o͝o). Note that there are a variety of spellings for each of these sounds.

(o͝o)				(u)		
book	look	took		moose	noose	loose
cook	hook	rook		dues	sues	rues
pull	full	wool		pool	fool	rule
foot	put	soot		suit	loot	hoot
would	could	should		do	new	who
stood	shook	woman		hoop	soup	loop
good	hood	wood		move	prove	lose

Practice Sentences with (o͝o) Sounds Capitalized

1. LOOk for the bOOk that you tOOk to school.
2. Did Lou pUll the wOOlen hOOd over Ruth's eyes?
3. You shOUld pUt your fOOt in the wOOly sock.
4. Sue's new suit wOUld lOOk gOOd on Lucy.
5. They stOOd in the soup line for a fUll hour.
6. PUt the ball through the hoop and you won't lose.
7. The freezing wOman shOOk and shivered, then pUlled the hOOd over her head.
8. Mr. FUller pUshed and pUlled but he cOUldn't open the wOOden door.
9. The cOOk tOOk a lOOk at the cOOkbOOk and shOOk more sUgar on the pUdding.
10. LOOk at the wOman who pUlled the loose noose off of the moose.
11. The gOOd bOOk stOOd on the bOOkshelf for years.
12. Mr. GOOdman tOOk a lOOk at the suit, but wOUldn't buy it.

Chapter 4: Word-Pronunciation Differences

Pronunciation differences commonly occur for particular words. The lessons in this chapter present the ones that are used most often.

For Get Forget Or Are Just The There A An To

Study the following pronunciation differences to determine how you pronounce these frequently used words:

	DIFFERENCE	GA/SE
for	fer, fuh, fo-uh	f-o-er
get	git, gih, geh	g-eh-t
forget	fergit, fuhget, fuhgih	f-o-er-geh-t
or	er, uh, o-uh	o-er
are	er, ah	ah-er
just	jis, jus, jes, jest	j-uh-st
the + consonant	thee boy, thee dog	th-uh boy, th-uh dog
the + vowel	thuh eye, thuh eggs	th-ee eye, th-ee eggs
there	ther, thay-uh	thay-er
a + consonant	ay girl, ay car	uh girl, uh car
an + vowel	uh apple, uh omelet	an apple, an omelet
to	tuh, tuhday, tuhnight	t-u

Read aloud the GA/SE pronunciations of these words until the pronunciation is comfortable and effortless. Practice the following sentences. DO NOT exaggerate the pronunciation of THE or A. The key words are capitalized.

1. JUST GET enough lemonade OR cola FOR THE weekend.
2. JUST FORGET about baking cookies OR A cake FOR A while.
3. THE intelligence of terriers is AN obvious trait.
4. THERE ARE A million stars out THERE TOnight in THE sky.
5. I went TO THE store FOR AN avocado but THERE was none.

6. Don't FORGET THE eggs and THE peppers FOR AN omelet.

7. Those ARE THE chairs that I bought FOR THE indoor pool.

8. JUST GET AN apple, AN orange, and A bunch of bananas.

9. JUST THE fact that THE teacher gave him AN A and me A B makes me FORGET how much I liked THE course.

10. JUST when I was about TO FORGET about him, THE ex-boyfriend sends me A card and AN antique ring FOR our anniversary. And, THERE ARE A dozen roses in my office!

11. Don't FORGET TO study History FOR THE exam TOmorrow.

12. If I FORGET TO GET AN illustrated story OR A mystery TO read TO THE children FOR THE inside recess, THERE will be complaints TOday and TOmorrow. JUST wait and see.

13. I JUST can't GET used TO THE fact that I don't have TO GET up at THE break of dawn.

14. I'm going TO say this FOR THE last time: don't FORGET TO clean THE kitchen, mow THE lawn, and walk THE dog.

15. If you ARE not A part of THE solution, then, you ARE A part of THE problem.

16. You JUST don't GET it!

17. THERE ARE A million things TO DO, so JUST do them.

18. AN apple, AN orange and AN ounce of good luck keeps THE doctor away.

19. I don't know whether I should GET tickets TO THE Bulls game, OR TO THE Sox game, OR TO THE Cubs game OR TO THE rap concert, OR TO THE opera.

20. THERE ARE A hundred reasons FOR GETTING JUST THE perfect person TO go with you TO AN exciting event OR A fancy party.

Fruit

The Broadcast/Standard English pronunciation of the word FRUIT is frustrating to some of you. As you practice the word list and sentences, remember NOT to substitute (f-you) for the words that begin with (f-ru) and vice versa.

f-you	f-ru
fff-you	fff-rrrrr-u
future	frugal
futile	fruity
few	fruit
fuse	fruitier
fuel	fruit fly
funeral	fruit cake
fugitive	fruition
fumes	fruitful
refute	frugality

Practice Sentences with Capitalized (fru) Sounds

1. You often feel futility about the future at a funeral.
2. Few people know how to change fuses and fuel.
3. The FRUit fly is FRUitful and multiplies FRUitfully.
4. Be FRUgal when buying FRUit cakes and dried FRUit.
5. Few people really like the fumes from FRUit cakes.
6. The lawyer refuted the fugitive's lies about the FRUit.
7. Few people think about the future, funerals and taxes.
8. Always wash the FRUit because a few might have chemical residue or FRUit flies.

Practice Paragraph with Capitalized (fru) Sounds

One day, a few of us went to Wisconsin to pick FRUit. We picked enough FRUit to fill six FRUit baskets. A few of the apples were rotten, but most of the FRUit was delicious. FRUit is healthy but FRUit is expensive. Because a few of us are FRUgal, we decided to sell the FRUit to a FRUit market for a profit. A few FRUit-stands bought our FRUit, and guess what a few of us did with our profits? Yes, we spent it all on juicy, FRUity, healthy FRUit!

"Different Pronunciations" List

Wanna try suh'm? Ahm gonna give ya somethin' tuh do an' ah wancha tuh see 'fya kin do it, an if iss easy fer yuh. Lessee how ya do!

Let's try that again.

DO YOU waNT TO try someTHING? I'm goING TO give yOU someTHING tO do. I wanT YOU tO see If yOU cAN do it, anD if iT's easy fOR yOU. LeT's see how yOU do!

The following list presents pronunciations of words and phrases that differ from the GA/SE style. None of us uses all of them, but most of us use some of them. The goal of this presentation is to help you determine which pronunciations you do use, and to introduce to you and/or review the SE alternatives. Turn to the appropriate lesson if you discover that you use a different pronunciation.

Words/ Phrases	Different Pronunciations	Phonetic GA/SE Pronunciation
a	ay boy, ay girl	uh boy, uh girl
an	a ear, a eye	an ear, an eye

(Pronounce the word, "a" as (uh); if it precedes a word that begins with a vowel, say, "an".)

the	thuh invitation	thEE invitation
the	thee boy	thUH boy

(When "the" precedes a word that begins with a vowel, say "thee"; before a consonant, say "thuh".)

it's	iss ok	iT's ok
what's	whass up?	whaT's up
that's	thass all	thaT's all
first	firs up	firST up
just	jes, jis, jus	juST
west	wesside	weST side

(continued)

Words/ Phrases	Different Pronunciations	Phonetic GA/SE Pronunciation
get	git me some	gEt me some
forget	forgit it	forgEt it
south	souf or sout	souTH side
north	norf or nort	norTH side
4th	forf or fort	fourTH grade
going to	fin', finna	I'm going to leave
getting ready to	–	I'm getting ready to leave
about to	–	I'm about to leave
and	an' I said	anD I said
should've	shoulda	should'uhV
could've	coulda	could'uhV
have to	hafta, gotta	haFF tO
had to	hadda	had tO
going to	gonna, go	goING TO
I'll	ahm-ah	I'm GOING TO
He'll	he-ah	He'S GOING TO
something	so'm, somethin	someTHING
nothing	nutt'n, nothin	noTHING
being	bein	beING
want to	wanna	waNT TO
don't	don, dun, do	doN'T do it
50 - 59	fitty-two...	fiFTy-two...
greasy	greezy	greaSy
police	PO-lice	puh-LEES
Detroit	DEE-troit	duh-TROIT

Words/ Phrases	Different Pronunciations	Phonetic GA/SE Pronunciation
says	sAYEEz	sehz
wash	wAHsh, wAWERsh	wAWsh
oil	AWl, ERl	OYuhl
himself	hisself	himself
can	kin, ken	I cAN do it
September	Set-ember	SePtember
kept	kep	I kePt it
ask	axe	ASS-K
asks	axis	ASS-KS
asked	axed, ast	ASS-KT
asking	axing	ASS-KING
Chicago	Chi-KAH-go	Chi-CAW-go
Illinois	Ell-i-noise	ILL-i-NOY
woman	wUH-min	wŎO-min (as in "book")
women	wUH-min	wIH-Min
kind of	kinna	kiND-UV
picture	pitcher	piCK-ture
library	li-berry	li-BRary
pumpkin	puN-Kin	puMP-kin
eggs	AYgz	EHgz
milk	mEL-k	mILL-k
100	hunnerd	hun-DRED
110	hunner'n ten	one hun-DRED ten

(continued)

Words/ Phrases	Different Pronunciations	Phonetic GA/SE Pronunciation
February	Feb-you-ary	Feb-ROO-ary
been	Ben	bin
for	fer	look f-OR it
or	er	OR I'll go
forget	fer-git	fOR-gEt it
there	thER	thAY-ER it is
I was	Ize	I WAS on the bus
said	He went, I went	He said, I said
says	He goes, I go	He says, I say
I	ah	AH-EE am happy
I'm	ahm, uhm	Ah-EEM tired
to	tuh	go TOO the store
today	tuh-day	it's hot TOO-day
tomorrow	tuh-morrow	I'll go TOO-morrow
anyway	anyways	Anyway, I can't.
sometimes	sometime	Sometimes, I can.
on	awn, õ	AHn

Final Practice Exam for SE Pronunciation

The following story contains many of the SE features that have been presented. As you read, record yourself so you can determine which features need more practice.

After Beth and Althea went shopping, they stopped at the first air-conditioned restaurant they noticed. Beth asked the waiter, "What's the best ice-cold drink on this list?" The waiter smiled and suggested, "A strained fruit juice drink is healthy and refreshing." Beth watched while another customer picked up something and finished it. "What's that?" she asked as she pointed to the customer's drink. "That's mashed banana juice," the waiter answered.

Beth grasped the menu and gazed down the list. Althea had been studying the whole list of cold desserts. She asked the waiter, "What's an 'Extra-Piled-On-High-Fudge-With-Ten-Kinds-Of-Ices'?" The waiter told her, "It's our most asked-for item." Beth's mouth watered, her lips trembled, and her eyes glazed. She risked gaining back all the pounds she had lost but she said, "Maybe I'll take one, with extra nuts!"

Beth gasped at Althea's choice. "And you, miss?" the waiter asked, looking at Beth. Beth laughed and said, "There are just too many desserts, drinks and lists on your menu. Perhaps we can share." Althea looked straight at Beth, and yelled, "That's the worst idea!" No sale, yet.

Just then, Mel and Len, the girls' male friends from high school, walked through the door. They recognized their old friends and asked, "What's happening?" as they reached to shake their hands. Mel and Len joined them at the table and asked, "Are you ordering drinks or ice cream?" The waiter complained, "No success, yet." "They can't decide by themselves, so I'll help," Mel announced. "She'll have," he said, pointing to Beth, "the excellent 'Chicago Fruity Special', and she'll have," he added, pointing to Althea, the extraordinarily delicious 'Illinois-Crushed-Fruit-Drink' with extra straws, extra spoons, and extra bibs," he laughed.

Excitedly, the waiter asked, "Anything for you?" Len answered, "We're so tired. We've exercised for ten hours, today. I don't want anything to eat, but Mel and I will share the 'One-Hundred-Fifty-Fruits-Juice' drink." Mel said, "He'll have that himself. I don't have to share. I kind of feel like the 'Fill-Up-With-Chilled-Lime-Things' and the same drink that Althea's having." "Perfect choices for a hot September afternoon," the waiter said. "It just takes a few moments to get," he added, "so enjoy yourselves!"

SECTION II: GRAMMATICAL DIFFERENCES

Dr. J. L. Dillard states in his book, *Black English*, that "grammar is ... used herein to mean not 'correct use of language,' but 'the way a language works.' In this sense, every language (and every 'dialect') has a grammar ..."

This section of *Speak Standard, Too* presents ways in which oral SE grammar differs from the grammatical systems of other English dialects. Grammatical differences do not illustrate one system's superiority over another. Grammatical features are contrasted to help heighten your awareness of what you need to do in order to acquire SE for use in school and at work. Remember that it is acceptable to continue to use your own dialect's grammar at home and with friends.

It is interesting to note how grammatical differences can influence pronunciation differences and vice versa. It was explained in the Introduction how most African and Asian languages do not change verb forms when they express past tense. It was also mentioned in the section on Pronunciation Differences, that most Asian languages and many West African languages do not end words with consonants, especially clusters of consonants. It makes sense, then, that people of African and Asian language backgrounds often omit final consonants, including the -ED ending, and reduce or omit consonant clusters. This results in both pronunciation and grammatical differences. For example:

  MISSED, pronounced MIST, loses (st) if pronounced MISS
  LOVED, pronounced LOVD, loses (vd) if pronounced LOVE
  BAKED, pronounced BAKT, loses (kt) if pronounced BAKE
  GAZED, pronounced GAZD, loses (zd) if pronounced GAZE

Listed below are the grammatical differences that have already been covered in the section on Pronunciation:

- "ed" endings for past-tense (page 12)
- "s" endings for plurals (pages 27 and 28)
- "s" endings for possessives (pages 27 and 29)
- "s" endings for third person singular present tense and contractions (pages 27, 30 and 33)

Choose your first grammatical difference from the Different Features list you made on page xv, and begin.

The POSITIVES and the NEGATIVES (Double Negatives)

SE uses single negatives. Other English dialects, like American BE, can use more than one negative in a sentence. A negative word expresses the concept of NO. All the N'T verbs like ISN'T and DON'T are negatives. NO ONE, NOBODY, NOTHING, NONE, NOT, and NEVER are also negatives.

NO is also a negative, of course, but in SE you do not count it when it occurs as the initial emphasis in a reply. Note these two examples:

Q: Do you want to buy some clothes?

A: No, I DON'T want to buy ANY clothes. (SE)

No, I DON'T want to buy NO clothes. (Double negative)

Q: Did you do any studying?

A: No, I DIDN'T do ANY studying. (SE)

No, I DIDN'T do NO studying. (Double negative)

Change the following double (or triple) negative sentences into single negative SE answers.

1. I'm not doing nothing.
2. I never go nowhere.
3. I don't never know nobody there.
4. I don't like no flashy clothes.
5. We can't never do nothing new.
6. Don't be no complainer.
7. They won't say nothing to no one.
8. You don't never have nothing to eat.
9. I can't take no kids to the movies.
10. My mom won't give me no allowance.

Begin with NO as you answer the following questions with SE single negative answers.

1. Do you have any brothers or sisters?

2. Are you doing anything important?

3. Are you going anywhere for a vacation?

4. Do you know anybody at this party?

5. Do you like lamb chops?

6. Do you want some chops for dinner?

7. Does this radio ever work?

8. Do you have a dog?

9. Will you please give me a watch for my birthday?

10. Have you ever received any parking tickets?

AIN'T Isn't Standard!

SE speakers do not use AIN'T. When AIN'T is used it replaces the various forms of be-verbs, as in "It AIN'T" for "It ISN'T." AIN'T also replaces the SE helping verbs like HAVE and HAS, as in "She AIN'T been here" for "She HASN'T been here." Which style do you use in the following sentence-pairs?

DIFFERENCE	SE
Ain't he funny?	Isn't he funny?
Ain't they glad?	Aren't they glad?
Ain't we working hard?	Aren't we working hard?
Ain't I handsome?	Aren't I handsome?
Ain't you going?	Aren't you going?
It ain't big.	It isn't big.
I ain't wrong.	I'm not wrong.
They ain't going.	They aren't going.
She ain't been home.	She hasn't been home.
We ain't been there.	We haven't been there.

Start each SE reply to the following questions with NO. Use single negatives (see page 82).

1. Ain't you been here before?
2. Ain't he a Sophomore?
3. Ain't Amena going with Isiah?
4. Ain't that car beautiful?
5. Ain't her name Maria?
6. Ain't he on the baseball team?
7. Ain't we finished?
8. Ain't those pictures pretty?

Change the following sentences into SE.

1. The weather ain't nice today.
2. It ain't warm and the sun ain't shining neither.
3. He ain't working so he ain't eating.
4. She ain't losing no weight.
5. Bob ain't no Shakespearean actor.
6. My friends ain't mad at me no more.

7. They ain't never taken me nowhere.

8. We ain't here just to fool around.

9. You ain't laughing at my jokes.

10. My classmates ain't never laughed at me.

11. His sister ain't mean to him.

12. Ain't no girl gonna tie me down.

13. Ain't no good food in this house.

14. Ain't no law against having fun.

15. There ain't no pencil near this phone.

Read the following sentences and note or circle the SE equivalents of "ain't."

1. There aren't enough tomatoes to make a salad.

2. They aren't coming with us tonight.

3. Susan isn't here yet.

4. I'm not having a good time.

5. Aren't you the same guy I met last night?

6. Isn't your name John?

7. Why isn't A.J. here?

8. Isn't Jay at practice?

9. Haven't you finished your paper yet?

10. Hasn't Martha seen that movie already?

Circle the SE be-verbs as you read this story out loud.

It's Saturday. There are no classes. Dan and Doug aren't doing anything. "Aren't you hungry?" Doug asks. "No," Dan answers, "I'm not hungry, I'm bored. Aren't you bored?" "No," Doug answers, "I'm not bored, I'm hungry." "Aren't we supposed to meet A.J. and Ryan for breakfast?" Dan asks. "No," Doug replies, "They're not here this week-end. Aren't you supposed to be at a science lab?" "No," Dan answers, "My professor isn't requiring labs anymore." "Isn't there a softball tournament today?" Doug asks. "No," Dan says, "There aren't enough people who signed up. And, there isn't even a concert tonight because the lead singer isn't in the band anymore."

"Let's get pizza," Doug suggests. "I don't have any money," Dan says. "I don't have any, either," Doug adds. "Well, there aren't any friends around, there isn't anything to do, and there isn't any money to do it with, anyway, so ... back to sleep!"

-ING Looking for IS or ARE

SE speakers use the be-verbs (AM, IS, and ARE) plus -ING verbs to describe a current ongoing action, as in "She IS studyING." Some English dialects, like American Black English, allow omission of IS and ARE when expressing an ongoing action, as in "She studying."

Study the following contrasting sentences in order to determine which type of -ING sentence you use. If you do not ordinarily use the SE style, practice the sentences until you feel more comfortable using IS and ARE with -ING verbs (pages 88 and 89 have more drills regarding IS and ARE).

BE	SE
She making dinner.	She's making dinner.
He cleaning up.	He's cleaning up.
They expecting company.	They're expecting company.
They worrying about it.	They're worrying about it.
What you doing?	What are you doing?
Where you going?	Where are you going?
He sleeping late.	He's sleeping late.
She getting up early.	She's getting up early.
We going out tonight.	We're going out tonight.
We hoping it'll rain.	We're hoping it'll rain.

Circle the -ING and be-verbs in the following SE sentences.

1. You are going to work early this morning.

2. Why are you going so early?

3. Are you trying to catch up on your files?

4. I'm sleeping late because I'm not worried.

5. We're going to see a movie tonight.

Change the following sentences to SE style.

1. He paying for you but he not treating me.

2. She reading a scary book and she not sleeping.

3. He mowing the lawn and his son planting the flowers.

4. They getting up early tomorrow to catch the train.

5. We wondering if you ever going to be ready.

6. Dan thinking that he should go home.

7. He talking on the phone now, so keep the noise down.

8. He working out at the gym now.

9. You going home, now?

10. She cooking us fish and she baking us cookies.

11. We going home now.

12. He trying to make the team.

13. He too tired to watch TV anymore.

14. They happy to be home.

15. You finished?

Circle the -ING and be-verbs as you read the following story out loud.

Ami is looking for a job. She's tired. She's frustrated. She's polite and attentive during the interview, but she's getting tired of hearing, "You're a terrific candidate, but you're not experienced enough."

Ami is also tired of talking to personnel managers. They are nice. They are polite. They are interested. They are always smiling. But, they are not offering her jobs.

Ami is saying to herself that she's so sick of being rejected that she's not going to go to another interview. Her friend, Lisa, is on the phone. She is telling Ami about a job in her company. "I'm so sick of this," she says, "but I guess I'll go to one more interview."

Ami is amazed. Ami is stunned. Ami is so happy. The interviewer is saying, "You are the perfect person for this job. It's yours!" Ami is on the phone with Lisa and she is screaming, "Tonight we are celebrating!"

There's Never a COPula When You Need One (Use of be-verbs)

SE uses IS and ARE (and AM) to connect the subjects of sentences with the nouns, pronouns and adjectives that relate to them. For example, in the sentences, "She IS happy" and "They ARE teachers," IS connects SHE with HAPPY and ARE connects THEY with TEACHERS. When IS and ARE are connectors, they are called copulas.

Not all English dialects use the be-verb copula. BE, for example, does not use IS and ARE as connectors. "She happy" and "They teachers" are acceptable BE sentences.

Study the following sentence-pairs in order to identify the SE style of using the copulas IS and ARE in present-tense sentences. (See pages 86 and 89 for more drills and information regarding IS and ARE usage.)

DIFFERENCE	SE
He lucky.	He's lucky.
She pretty.	She's pretty.
She six years old.	She's six years old.
We ready.	We're ready.
Jenny smart.	Jenny's smart.
Tom big and smart.	Tom is big and smart.
Our daddy tall.	Our daddy's tall.
George a soldier.	George is a soldier.

Add the SE copulas to each of the following sentences.

1. We glad that he happy with my work.

2. He so handsome that he a model.

3. We too late to take the train to New York.

4. She only six years old but she a good reader.

5. They all eighth grade teachers.

6. We all too tired to stay up late.

7. It too hot today to study.

8. We almost through with these reference books.

9. They in Lincoln School all day, and then they in the Sunshine Day Care Center.

10. They happy that we not late.

Be Agreeable with AM, IS, ARE, WAS, WERE (Subject agreement with be-verbs)

In some English dialects, the verb always "agrees" with the subject without changing the verb's ending. For example, in American BE, "I do" and "He do" are both correct. SE, however, is irregular in its subject-verb agreement. The SE speaker says "I do" and then must change the verb for "He doES." (Drills on subject-verb agreement are found throughout Section II.) We are now going to focus on how to make the subject of a SE sentence agree with the be-verbs AM, IS, ARE, WAS and WERE.

The following are conjugations of the be-verb in the present tense and the past tense. Note in the chart below how and when each verb changes in order to "agree" with its subject pronoun.

PRESENT TENSE		PAST TENSE	
I AM	We ARE	I WAS	We WERE
You ARE	You ARE	You WERE	You WERE
He, She, It IS	They ARE	He, She, It WAS	They WERE

Study the following sentence-pairs. Try to determine when you use the SE style and/or the different style.

SE	DIFFERENCE
I AM not going to go.	I is not going to go.
You ARE doing well.	You is doing well.
He IS busy.	He busy.
She IS taking Speech.	She am taking Speech.
It IS hot.	It hot.
We ARE ready.	We is ready.
They ARE exercising.	They is exercising.
The boy IS hungry.	The boy hungry.
Janie IS tired.	Janie tired.
The radio IS on.	The radio, it on.
Our fans ARE loyal.	Our fans is loyal.
They ARE so honest.	They is so honest.
I AM so excited.	Im am so excited.
Where ARE they?	Where is they?
ARE you busy?	Is you busy?
We'RE not ready.	We's not ready.
They'RE too early.	They's too early.

Below you will find exercises that will help you to begin to acquire the SE agreement of subjects with be-verbs. As you do the exercises, make sure that the subjects and be-verbs AGREE according to the conjugation chart on the preceding page.

Practice getting agreeable with be-verbs.

Using both the present and past tense forms of be-verbs, describe the members of your family. First, say it out loud, then write down exactly what you said.

  1. My mom (is a generous person.) (was a generous person.)

  2. She _____

  3. My dad _____

  4. He _____

  5. My sister(s) _____

  6. She or They _____

  7. My brother(s) _____

  8. He or They _____

  9. My cousins _____

10. My aunt _____

11. My uncle _____

Describe the characteristics or actions of the following people and objects. Use the present and past tense of the be-verbs to do so. Check the conjugation chart.

  1. President Kennedy _____

  2. Mayor Washington _____

  3. The kids of today _____

  4. My friends and I _____

  5. I _____

  6. My classmates _____

  7. You and the others _____

  8. Chicago _____

If you think it is necessary, change the WAS or WERE verbs so that the following sentences are in the SE style of speaking. Refer to the conjugation charts on page 89 to confirm your answers.

1. Was your parents at church Sunday?

2. Rodney and Tanya wasn't in school.

3. Were Beverly and Ed good friends last year?

4. Was Muhammad and Susan inflecting their voices or was they speaking in monotones?

5. What was you doing out until midnight last night?

6. Tony was unhappy because the kids was being mean.

7. Christy and Lynetta was working on their (th) sounds.

8. John was married last week and his bride and he were so happy.

9. Was Kenyatta and Peter working at the department store?

10. June was cleaning the house until her three friends called and said they was going to the beach.

11. Sweaters was on sale for $25.99.

12. The raspberries and blueberries was so delicious.

13. You was mean to say those things to me.

14. My classmates were so nice to me.

15. Tell me what you was doing at nine o'clock on Thursday.

16. My aunts and uncles was so happy to see me.

17. The videos that I rented were excellent but sad.

18. They was always out for a good time – nothing else.

19. We wasn't going to stay as long as we did.

20. We weren't happy about the way things turned out.

You're BE-ING Repetitive

Another grammatical form that differs from SE is the one that uses "be" + ING verbs or adjectives to express a situation that occurs repetitively. Some English speakers can say, "I BE TIRED all the time." The SE speaker's equivalent to that is "I AM tired all the time." The Black English speaker who says, "I BE watchING TV" usually means the same as the SE speaker's "I WATCH TV," not "I am watching TV, now."

Read aloud the following sentence-pairs until you feel comfortable with the SE counterpart to BE-ING repetitive.

DIFFERENCE	SE
He be riding the bus a lot.	He rides the bus a lot.
They be late every day.	They are late every day.
We be working Sundays.	We work on Sundays.
They always be open.	They always are open.
I be studying hard at school.	I study hard at school.

Change the BE-ING repetitive sentences to SE style.

1. I always be tired when I come home from work.

2. You never know what he be doing.

3. Tom always be making us laugh.

4. Sometimes we be having fun, and sometimes we be bored.

5. They be going for groceries every Tuesday night.

6. My baby be crying every morning between 4 and 6 A.M.

7. I know it just bes that way some times.

8. He be so sad all the time – I don't know what to do.

9. We be talking and laughing every day on the phone.

10. Caroline be getting A's every semester.

11. Car showrooms never be open on Sundays.

12. He never be watching TV anymore.

The "be" can also be used to express future tense. Read aloud the following sentence-pairs, which contrast SE's expression of the future with the "be" style.

DIFFERENCE	SE
He be in class soon.	He'll be in class soon.
We be leaving tomorrow.	We'll be leaving tomorrow.
I be too busy Tuesday.	I'll be too busy Tuesday.

Change the following future tense be-sentences to SE.

1. He be seeing you at work on Monday.
2. Where you be tomorrow at six o'clock?
3. I be waiting for you when class is over.
4. Dan be the Varsity point guard next year.
5. Ami be getting a job when she gets to Boston.
6. Linda be waiting in the check out line when she be finished with her shopping.
7. He never be calling if he be out of town all the time.
8. We always be going on vacation when school is finished.
9. David be graduating this coming June.
10. Life be easier when summer vacation starts.

Read the following sentences out loud and circle the SE verbs.

1. Sandra always walks her little sister home from school.
2. Robin baby-sits every Tuesday.
3. Everyone watches TV after dinner on Thursday nights.
4. She always thinks she's going to get a better grade than everyone else in the class and she never does.
5. She's always late because she takes too much time choosing which clothes she will wear.
6. It's not easy to study for four hours every night.
7. Liza takes dancing lessons on Saturdays.
8. Sammy always sneaks a cookie out of the cookie jar when he comes home from school.
9. You never pay attention in class when the teacher gives the homework assignments.
10. Carla and Therese always stop for candy bars and eat them on the way home from work.

AH WILL Predict the Future (will or 'LL)

On the preceding page we discussed how "be" can express the future in BE dialect. BE and SE speakers also use WILL, or its contraction, 'LL, to express the future, as in "He WILL (He'LL) go there tomorrow." If the BE speaker omits final (L) sounds, the pronunciation of 'LL sounds like (ah), as in "He-AH go there tomorrow."

Study the following sentence-pairs so you learn how to produce SE future-tense sentences using WILL or 'LL. (If you are having any difficulty making the (L) sound for the 'LL or WILL, see pages 36 and 54.)

DIFFERENCE	SE
She-ah start work on Monday.	She'll start work on Monday.
I-ah be going Tuesday.	I'll be going Tuesday.
They-ah be graduating soon.	They'll be graduating soon.
We-ah see her tomorrow.	We'll see her tomorrow.

Change the following sentences to SE style.

1. He-ah go when he's ready.

2. She-ah be worrying for days about her grades.

3. I-ah go back to work in January.

4. She-ah quit her job in September for school.

5. You-ah need your bank book to withdraw money.

6. He-ah be finished with his paper tonight.

7. When my mother gets back, we-ah leave.

8. When I graduate, I-ah get my own place.

9. When my dad is through, he-ah get us ice cream.

10. They-ah be teasing me if I don't pass Driver's Ed.

11. I-ah be so happy when summer comes.

12. She-ah change her work hours during vacation.

13. We-ah be getting tickets for the concert.

14. He said he-ah call me next Monday.

Being Agreeable with SAY, DO, DON'T, HAVE

If it seems as though we keep returning to subject-verb agreement, we do. It is important to develop some familiarity with this grammatical form if you are going to use SE with increased comfort and confidence.

This lesson helps you practice how to use SAY, DO, DON'T and HAVE in SE style. First, study the conjugation charts below. Notice which verb-endings change to S or ES.

SAY	DO	DON'T	HAVE
I say, We say	I do, We do	I don't, We don't	I have, We have
You say, You say	You do, You do	You don't, You don't	You have, You have
He says, They say	He does, They do	He doesn't, They don't	He has, They have
She says	She does	She doesn't	She has
It says	It does	It doesn't	It has

Study the following sentence-pairs. Which column contains the SE sentences? Check back with the conjugation charts to confirm your choice.

He always says that.	He always say that.
She never does it correctly.	She never do it correctly.
It has three parts to it.	It have three parts to it.
We do it all the time.	We does it all the time.
John has a big house.	John have a big house.
They all do well.	They all does well.
The radio has static.	The radio have static.
How does she do it?	How do she do it?
It doesn't work.	It don't work.
He doesn't care.	He don't care.
She doesn't travel.	She don't travel.

In the following sentences, IF NECESSARY, change the capitalized verbs in order to make the subject agree with the verb in the SE style. Refer to the conjugation charts above if you need to.

1. He SAY, "Please don't yell."

2. That TV always HAVE a bad picture.

3. She SAYS that she's very happy in her apartment.

4. It just DON'T seem right.

5. DO she always have to boss me around?

6. DOESN'T she look beautiful?

7. My mom DON'T allow me to stay out late.

8. Terry always SAY that his feet hurt.

9. That sign SAY, "Stop," so he HAVE to stop.

10. My sister never HAVE the "right" thing to wear.

11. I DOESN'T always know how to do my math problems.

12. They HAS to move to California.

13. We DON'T go out on the weekends anymore.

14. You DON'T seem to know where you're going.

15. My husband DON'T ask for directions when we're lost.

16. He SAY, "I DON'T HAVE to ask anybody for help."

Change the capitalized verbs so that they agree with their subjects in the SE style.

Every night my best friend SAY, "Let's go out." He DON'T go to school so he DON'T have to study. I SAYS to him that he HAVE to forget about me going out every night with him. He SAY, "Dan HAVE lots of homework and he DON'T stay home." I SAYS, "I DOESN'T care about what Dan DO or what he DON'T do – this guy only GO out on weekends."

Read the following story out loud; note the capitalized SE subjects and verbs.

PHILLIP SAYS that HE DOESN'T want to be in the senior musical. HE SAYS that HE HAS too many things to do. HE HAS homework, HE HAS a part-time job, HE HAS to finish his college applications, and HE HAS a chance to make the varsity basketball team. His FRIENDS SAY that HE DOESN'T have too much to do, and if HE DOESN'T have the musical as a Senior Year memory, he'll regret it. TONIE, his girlfriend, HAS the same opinion. SHE SAYS that if HE DOESN't join the cast, THEY HAVE no chance to be together because SHE HAS a part in it, too.

PHILLIP SAYS to himself that if HE DOES his homework at night, and if HE DOES his college applications on the weekends, then HE HAS enough time to rehearse after school. HE HAS to work 8 hours a week, but HE always HAS a choice as to when to work those hours. HE DOES want to play basketball, but COACH SAYS that tryouts start after the musical is over. So, PHILLIP SAYS to his friends that THEY DON'T have to worry because HE DOES have the time to be in the musical. HE SAYS, "I hope that I HAVE the lead role." "No way," THEY SAY, "YOU HAVE a terrible singing voice, YOU DON'T know how to dance, and YOU SAY lines as though YOU HAVE stones in your mouth. WE SAY that YOU HAVE to be in the chorus!"

HAVE You BEEN With HAS?

SE speakers always say HAVE or HAS (or HAD) before BEEN. You know how to make HAVE and HAS agree with their subjects in SE style (page 95). You also know that 'S at the end of a sentence-subject can stand for IS or HAS (page 33). Read aloud the following sentence-pairs. Decide which column contains the SE sentences; decide which style you usually use. Note that 'VE stands for HAVE, and 'D stands for HAD.

DIFFERENCE	SE
He been there before.	He has been there before.
She been to one movie.	She's been to one movie.
We been to the store.	We have been to the store.
I been to Mary's house.	I've been to Mary's house.
It been raining all day.	It's been raining all day.
They been away all day.	They'd been away all day.
My puppy been good.	My puppy's been good.
This been a bad night.	This has been a bad night.
You been sleeping?	Have you been sleeping?
Been busy?	Have you been busy?

Read the following sentences and change the verbs if they are not SE style.

1. I'VE BEEN gone so long, I can't remember her name.

2. He BEEN an excellent student all semester.

3. We HAVE BEEN meaning to call her for days.

4. I'D BEEN working at the bank for a year when I quit.

5. Mary'S BEEN taking French for six years.

6. You'VE always BEEN so nice to my family.

7. We BEEN having parties every weekend.

8. Junior year in high school HAS BEEN fun.

9. Applying to college HAVE not BEEN fun.

10. Jenny BEEN dating Dan for weeks when he broke it off.

11. We BEEN eating here for fifteen years.

12. Mitzi and Harold BEEN married for sixty years!

THEY Do THEIR Homework THEMSELVES (Possessive and Reflexive Pronouns)

SE uses THEY only as a sentence subject or after a be-verb; it uses THEIR to show possession; it uses THEM as an object or reflexive pronoun. Some English dialects use pronouns in a more regularized manner and THEY is used as the subject, the possessive, and the reflexive pronouns. For example:

	SE	DIFFERENCE
Subject	THEY went to the movies.	THEY went to the movies.
Be-Verbs	Are THEY the ones?	Are THEM the ones?
Possessive	THEIR dog ran away.	THEY dog ran away.
Reflexive	They fixed it THEMselves.	They fixed it THEYselves.
	They'll do it THEMselves.	They'll do it THEIRselves.

Read the following sentence-pairs so you can determine which pronouns you usually use to show possession and reflexiveness for THEY. Study them again so that you can begin to feel comfortable using THEIR and THEMSELVES. Note that, in addition to the regularized THEY, other pronoun differences are contrasted. Do you use any of them?

DIFFERENCE	SE
That's they house.	That's their house.
They built it theyselves.	They built it themselves.
He's they father.	He's their father.
She's they mother.	She's their mother.
They love they school.	They love their school.
They walk by theirself.	They walk by themselves.
They have they own store.	They have their own store.
The kids help they parents.	The kids help their parents.
Tom likes to eat by hisself.	Tom likes to eat by himself.
Jim wrote the paper hisself.	Jim wrote the paper himself.

Read aloud the following SE sentences. Note the capitalized usage of THEY, THEIR and THEMSELVES. How would you say these sentences in your own style?

1. THEY want to buy a new car, but THEIR parents disagree.

2. THEY went to THEIR cousin's house by THEMSELVES.

3. THEY bought THEIR uniforms by THEMSELVES.

4. Sandy and Tom went to California by THEMSELVES.

5. THEY loved THEIR hotel and THEIR room.

6. THEIR friends, Carol and Nick, visited THEIR hotel.

7. THEY ate by THEMSELVES every night in THEIR room.

8. THEY lost THEIR suitcases at the airport.

9. The kids built THEIR lemonade stand by THEMSELVES.

10. THEY lost THEIR books on THEIR way to school.

11. We need THEIR help and THEIR money.

12. THEY built THEIR garage by THEMSELVES.

13. THEY used to eat by THEMSELVES in THEIR favorite coffee shop every Wednesday night.

14. THEY traveled by THEMSELVES because THEY were afraid that THEIR vacations would be ruined if THEY made travel plans with THEIR friends.

15. Why don't THEY ever invite us to THEIR home?

16. THEIR basketball team was much better than THEIR soccer team.

17. We passed by THEIR new house and saw that THEY were doing the landscaping THEMSELVES.

18. THEY told THEIR customers that if THEY were not able to install the tiles THEMSELVES, THEY would give them THEIR own training sessions.

19. THEY were so frustrated with THEIR team's losses, that the fans ran out on THEIR gym floor and started to play THEMSELVES.

20. Janie is THEIR aunt; Leon is THEIR uncle; and Jackie, Jill and Ross are THEIR cousins.

21. THEY attended THEIR school for fourteen years and so did most of THEIR friends.

22. THEY were well-prepared for college because THEY did most of THEIR high school homework by THEMSELVES.

23. THEY watch each other so THEY can learn how to tie THEIR shoelaces by THEMSELVES.

24. THEY are going to lose THEIR hearing and THEIR parents are going to lose THEIR patience if THEY don't turn down the volume of THEIR music.

25. THEY are beginning to understand the value of THEIR education and how it will help them support THEIR families and allow them to function by THEMSELVES without the help of THEIR parents.

That's WHERE It's AT!

SE speakers are not supposed to use the word AT when WHERE is in the sentence. Read the following sentence-pairs and decide WHERE the SE sentences ARE.

Where's my notebook at?	Where's my notebook?
Where's your car at?	Where's your car?
Where's your house at?	Where's your house?
Wherever she's at, I'll find her.	Wherever she is, ...
Where's your mom at?	Where's your mom?
Where's it at?	Where is it?

Change the following sentences into the SE style where necessary.

1. Where we at?

2. Where's the party at?

3. Where they at?

4. Where are they now?

5. When you're defending, know where your man is at.

6. It's 10:30. Do you know where your teenager's at?

7. Where's that movie playing?

8. Where's the el stop at?

9. I hope he's happy wherever he's at.

10. Always know where your house keys're at.

11. Where's my Standard English Speech Manual?

MOTHER GOOSE & GRIMM

THERE'RE, IT'S and THERE'S

This lesson covers two related grammatical styles that differ from SE. The first difference is the very common usage of THERE'S instead of THERE'RE. Related to that difference is a usage more common among BE speakers: using IT'S instead of the SE words THERE'S and THERE'RE.

First, SE speakers use THERE'S when it refers to something that is singular, as in "THERE'S my dog." THERE'RE is used when it refers to more than one thing, as in "THERE'RE my dogs." A common grammatical difference occurs when the singular form is substituted for the plural. For example:

SE Singular	There's my neighbor.	There's one man here.
SE Plural	There're my neighbors.	There're two men here.
Difference	There's my neighbors.	There's two men here.

In addition to using IT as a pronoun that refers to one object, a BE speaker might use IT for the same reason that a SE speaker uses THERE – as a word, without meaning, that starts some sentences. For example:

BE	It's thirteen kids in my class.
SE	There're thirteen kids in my class.

BE	It's one more math problem to do.
SE	There's one more math problem to do.

If necessary, change the following sentences to SE.

1. It's a store on Chicago Avenue that I like.

2. There's so many rides to go on at Great America.

3. There's too many students in my Speech class.

4. There are so many bank employees from my school.

5. It's a lot of people in front of me in this line.

6. It's a sweater on my chair that you can borrow.

7. There's so many places where we could eat tonight.

8. There're so many good videos that we could rent.

9. It's a lot of noise on my block on Saturday night.

Answer the following questions in SE style.

1. How many people ARE THERE in your family?

2. IS THERE noise on Orchard Street at night?

3. How many apartments ARE THERE in that building?

4. How many questions ARE THERE on this sheet?

5. How many kids ARE THERE in your Speech class?

6. IS THERE a store on State Street that sells sweaters?

7. IS THERE a good book that you would like to read?

8. ARE THERE at least two female doctors in this hospital?

You're REPEATING Yourself (Double Subject)

SE speakers mention the subject of a sentence once. BE speakers, as well as others, repeat the sentence subject in another form in order to give it their dialect's grammatically required emphasis. For example:

SE	My MOTHER's a teacher.
BE	My MOTHER, SHE's a teacher.

SE	That BOY is my little brother.
BE	That BOY, HE is my little brother.

If subject-repetition-for-emphasis is part of your speaking style, study the following sentence-pairs in order to become familiar with the SE alternative.

SE	DIFFERENCE
Your dad is so smart .	Your dad, he's so smart.
My best friend is funny.	My best friend, she's funny.
My son just graduated.	My son, he just graduated.
That puppy is so soft.	That puppy, it's so soft.
His wife is a lawyer.	His wife, she's a lawyer.
Dan is not here today.	Dan, he's not here today.

Read the following two stories. Change the repeated sentence subjects to SE style.

1. Every week my friend, she says, "Let's go on a vacation to Florida." My friend, her name's LaJuana. LaJuana, she thinks I can go anywhere I want to go. My mom, she thinks I should go with LaJuana, but my dad, he thinks I should stay home and send my mom and him to Florida!

2. That man over there behind the desk, he's Mr. Smith. Mr. Smith, he's my boss. He's also Jane's boss. Jane and I, we think he's a tyrant. We call him "General." The two of us, we pretend to stand at attention when he calls for us. And "General," he just salutes and marches by!

As you read the third story, circle the unrepeated SE sentence subjects.

3. That woman is my son's fourth-grade teacher. Mrs. Feller is so nice. My son stays after school to help her. Mrs. Feller gives him little jobs to do. My son washes the black board and empties the wastebaskets. His teacher says that the classroom is so clean. His bedroom sure isn't!

The Gruesome Twosome: GOT and GOTTA
The Perfect Couple: HAVE and HAVE TO

In SE, HAVE and HAS are used to communicate ownership in the present tense. GOT is used as a past tense form for GET. A grammatical difference occurs when English speakers use GOT to mean HAVE/HAS. For example:

SE	You HAVE a dog. (You own a dog.)
SE	You GOT a dog. (You acquired a dog yesterday)
Diff.	You GOT a dog. (You own a dog.)

In addition, many English speakers substitute GOTTA for the SE phrase HAVE TO when they want to express that something is necessary. For example:

SE	I HAVE TO study for my English exam.
Diff.	I GOTTA study for my English exam.

The following sentence-pairs demonstrate these differences. First, try to determine what your word choices are. Then, read the SE sentences aloud so that you establish some comfort using the new style. (Note that the SE pronunciation of HAVE TO is HAF TO.)

DIFFERENCE	SE
You got a lot to do.	You have a lot to do.
I gots an apple for lunch.	I have an apple for lunch.
They got a new car.	They have a new car.
I got a good book to read.	I have a good book to read.
You gotta go home now.	You have to go home now.
We gotta walk the dog.	We have to walk the dog.
He's gotta study tonight.	He has to study tonight.
They gotta leave now.	They have to leave now.
Ami's gotta clean up.	Ami has to clean up.
Anyone got a pencil?	Does anyone have a pencil?

Change the following sentences to SE style.

1. You gotta go now because I got a lot of studying to do.

2. He's gotta clean up because we got company coming soon.

3. Sandy gots lots of friends from college.

4. Ben's gotta balance the books before he goes home.

5. Mary got that sweater yesterday, but she's gotta get another one because she's got a house in Vermont.

6. I gotta get some good seats for the Stones concert.

7. There's something I gotta tell you.

8. Dan's got an amazing collection of baseball cards.

9. They gotta get out of here or I got big trouble.

10. I gotta say that you got a lot of nerve coming here.

Beware: Irregular Past Participles

SE has regular and irregular verbs. The SE speaker adds an -ED ending to regular verbs to communicate the past; the entire word is changed to express the past tense of an irregular verb. For example:

SE Reg. Verb   Today, I walk.   Yesterday, I walkED.
SE Irreg. Verb   Today, I write.   Yesterday, I WROTE.

When SE speakers talk about an event that went on for a while and may still be ongoing, HAVE-HAS-HAD are followed by the main verb. If the main verb is a regular verb, the -ED ending is added; if the main verb is an irregular verb, a predetermined form of the verb is used. This tense is sometimes called PAST PARTICIPLE. For example:

Reg.   Yesterday, I walkED.   I HAVE walkED many times.
Irreg. Yesterday, She WROTE.   She HAS WRITTEN many times.

Differences occur if speakers omit the HAVE-HAS-HAD, but still use the SE participial form of the verb:

Diff.   I SUNG that song.
SE   I HAVE SUNG that song.

Differences also occur if the speaker uses the HAVE-HAS-HAD, but adds the past tense verb, not the SE participle:

Diff.   She HAS BEGAN to cry.
SE   She HAS BEGUN to cry.

Some English speakers use BEEN instead of the SE use of HAVE-HAS-HAD + BEEN (see page 97):

Diff.   He BEEN there before.
SE   He HAS BEEN there before.

Another difference exists when the speaker uses BEEN + VERB instead of the SE style of HAVE-HAS-HAD + BEEN + VERB:

Diff.   They BEEN GONE a day.
SE   They HAVE BEEN GONE a day.

Some speakers use the SE participle as the past tense:

Diff.   He DONE the work.
SE   He DID the work.

DONE is sometimes used instead of the SE HAVE-HAS-HAD to begin the participle:

Diff.   He DONE SEEN her.
SE   He HAS SEEN her.

Finally, some English dialects, including BE, allow DID to be used as a participle:

Diff.   He DONE DID the dishes.
SE   He HAS DONE the dishes.

The following word lists contain common irregular verbs. If you memorize the way the verbs change for the past tense and the past participle, you will begin to feel more confident about using them in the SE style.

PRESENT	PAST	PAST PARTICIPLE
begin	began	have/has begun
break	broke	have/has broken
come	came	have/has come
do	did	have/has done
drink	drank	have/has drunk
give	gave	have/has given
go	went	have/has gone
ride	rode	have/has ridden
ring	rang	have/has rung

(continued)

PRESENT	PAST	PAST PARTICIPLE
run	ran	have/has run
see	saw	have/has seen
speak	spoke	have/has spoken
swim	swam	have/has swum
take	took	have/has taken
throw	threw	have/has thrown
write	wrote	have/has written

Study the following sentence-pairs. Try to determine if you use any of the forms that are contrasted with the SE style. Try to say the equivalent SE sentence before you look at it.

DIFFERENCE	SE
He have swam six lengths.	He HAS SWUM six lengths.
He swum at the beach.	He SWAM at the beach.
She rung the dinner bell.	She RANG the dinner bell.
They have tooken it away.	They HAVE TAKEN it away.
You done did your paper.	You HAVE DONE your paper.
He been to Florida.	He HAS BEEN to Florida.
He throwed it away.	He THREW it away.
We have rode in his car.	We HAVE RIDDEN in his car.
He done his chores.	He DID his chores.
I've wrote her a letter.	I'VE WRITTEN her a letter.
He come late to the party.	He CAME late to the party.
She done ran to the bus.	She HAS RUN to the bus.
Something have went wrong.	Something HAS GONE wrong.
They've rang the bell.	They'VE RUNG the bell.

Practice Sentences for IRREGULAR VERBS: PAST TENSE and PAST PARTICIPLE

Fill in the blanks of each of the following sentences with SE past tense and past participle verbs. After you complete the drill, check your answers with the lists of verbs on the preceding two pages.

Verbs

do	1. I finally have _____ the assignment that Janie _____ last month.
come	2. Mom _____ home an hour ago, but Dad hasn't _____ home yet.
drink	3. She _____ more cola last night than she has _____ in a week.
write	4. Ami _____ more letters from Boston this summer than she had _____ all year.
see	5. They _____ the most beautiful parrot that they had ever _____.
swim	6. I _____ in the same pool in which Mark Spitz has _____ every day this week.
take	7. You should have _____ the class I _____.
ring	8. The telephone _____ off the hook yesterday, but it hasn't _____ at all today.
run	9. I _____ every day last week, but I haven't _____ today.
go	10. Ed _____ to Sam's, but Sam had _____ .
throw	11. Dan _____ Gavin the same ball that Gavin had _____ to him.
speak	12. I _____ to Ami last Thursday, but I haven't _____ to her since then.
begin	13. Nan _____ to study Monday, but she should have _____ on Friday.

GONNA – GON – GOING TO

What're you GONNA do today? I'm GON study all night. What you GON do? I'm GONNA brush my dog, and them I'm GONNA watch TV.

You not GON study, and you're not GONNA watch TV.

You ARE GOING TO learn how to use the SE counterpart to GON and GONNA. Read the following sentence-pairs and determine which form of GOING TO you use most frequently. Read the sentence-pairs again so that you become more familiar with the SE style. (See page 94 for AH and future tense.)

DIFFERENCE	SE
They gon play outside.	They ARE GOING TO play outside.
We all gon play ball.	We ARE all GOING TO play ball.
Dan's gonna wash the car.	Dan'S GOING TO wash the car.
I'm gonna watch a video.	I'M GOING TO watch a video.
You gon sleep late?	ARE you GOING TO sleep late?
No, I'm gonna get up early.	No, I'M GOING TO get up early.
He gon get an A.	He'S GOING TO get an A.

The following paragraph is an exercise for using GOING TO. First, read the paragraph aloud and exaggerate the capitalized words. Then, choose the word you usually use – GON or GONNA – and read the passage again, exaggerating the different usage. Read the paragraph for a third time and use the SE version in an unexaggerated and natural-sounding style.

I am so tired that I AM GOING TO go to sleep early tonight. Edward'S GOING TO meet me at the Athenian Room, and we'RE GOING TO eat Greek chicken. Then we'RE GOING TO walk home. Marty and Bonnie ARE probably GOING TO come over for coffee and cake. If it's nice outside, we'RE GOING TO sit out on our porch. I bet that my neighbors ARE GOING TO ask Edward to play his banjo, but he told me that he'S GOING TO have to do some work. At 10 o'clock, I'M GOING TO say, "Good-night, folks!" and then, I'M GOING TO go to bed. What ARE you GOING TO do?

Answer the paragraph's last question by telling yourself, out loud, at least ten things that you are GOING TO DO tonight and tomorrow.

THEM or THOSE?

In SE, THEM is a pronoun-object, as in "I like THEM."

It is also part of the reflexive pronoun, THEMSELVES (see page 98). It cannot describe nouns the way an adjective does. SE uses THESE and THOSE to describe nouns. Differences occur when speakers use THEM instead of THOSE. For example:

SE	THOSE BOOKS are expensive.	I like THOSE KIDS.
Diff.	Them books are expensive.	I like them kids.

Study the following sentence-pairs. If you determine that you use THEM as an adjective, read the sentence-pairs again until you feel more comfortable using THOSE to describe nouns.

DIFFERENCE	SE
Them guys are strong.	THOSE guys are strong.
Show me them pictures.	Show me THOSE pictures.
Do you like them shoes?	Do you like THOSE shoes.
Them slacks are expensive.	THOSE slacks are expensive.
Them kids are smart.	THOSE kids are smart.
Watch out for them rocks.	Watch out for THOSE rocks.

Change the following sentences into SE sentences.

1. Watch out for them potholes!
2. Them tires are all flat.
3. Them books are too long.
4. Tell them kids to be quiet.
5. Count them invoices before you go to lunch.
6. "How about them Bulls?"
7. Keep them dogs out of my yard.
8. I think we can beat all them other teams.
9. Where did you buy them sweaters?
10. Them are the ones I want.
11. I need them reports on my desk, now.
12. Them guys are just too loud for this restaurant.

Choosing ME or I

When do we use I and other subject pronouns? When do we use ME and other object pronouns? If you are not always sure about the answer, you share that lack of confidence with most English-speaking Americans. Test yourself. Choose which of the columns below contains the SE pronouns.

Just between you and me ...	Just between you and I...
Come with Pete and me.	Come with Pete and I.
This is she speaking.	This is her speaking.
Yes, it's I.	Yes, it's me.
Don is as smart as I.	Don is as smart as me.
Do you know Pam and him?	Do you know Pam and he?
Janie and I went shopping.	Janie and me went shopping.
Jim's taller than I.	Jim's taller than me.
You and I should go now.	Me and you should go now.

Did you think that the SE sentences were in the second column until you got to about the sixth sentence? Then, you may have correctly identified Column 1 as the SE sentences. The rules and techniques listed below will help you become more confident about your choice of SE pronouns.

Rule A. I, HE, SHE, WE, THEY (and YOU) are DOERS. They are the sentence subjects which DO the action or THINK. They also come after be-verbs. For example:

HE GOES home.	SHE GOES home.	HE and SHE GO home.
WE KNOW.	THEY KNOW.	THEY and WE KNOW.
SHE THINKS.	I THINK.	SHE and I THINK.
Who IS SHE?	Who IS HE?	Who ARE HE and SHE?
HE WORKS.	I WORK.	HE and I WORK.

Rule B. ME, HIM, HER, US, THEM (and YOU) are DOEES. The action of the verb is DONE to them; they also come after the prepositions. For example:

You HIT HIM.	You HIT ME.	You HIT HIM and ME.
Ride WITH HER.	Ride WITH ME.	Ride WITH HER and ME.
He HURT THEM.	He HURT ME.	He HURT THEM and ME.
Run to HER.	Run TO HIM.	Run TO HER and HIM.
Look AT HER.	Look AT ME.	Look AT HER and ME.

Rule C. If you are not sure about which pronoun to use, take out the other names and pronouns in the sentence; if it is necessary, change the verb in order to test each pronoun, and you will know immediately which SE pronoun to use. For example:

Test Sentence #1:   Him and me fixed it for her.

Test for HIM:	Him/He fixed it for her.	(He)
Test for ME:	Me/I fixed it for her.	(I)
Test for HER:	He and I fixed it for her/she.	(her)
SE Sentence:	He and I fixed it for her.	

Test Sentence #2:   Him and her like Pete and I.

Test for HIM:	Him/he likes Pete and I.	(He)
Test for HER:	Her/she likes Pete and I.	(She)
Test for I:	He and she like I/me.	(me)
SE Sentence:	He and she like Pete and me.	

Rule D. Say names before pronouns; say ME, I, US, WE last.

Robert and he went with John and her.
Justin and she went with Daniel and them.

Rule E. Use the DOER pronouns after THAN, AS, and be-verbs:

She's taller THAN I. He's smarter THAN SHE.
They're as sad AS I. The winner IS HE.

Use the DOEE pronouns after LIKE:

She's tall LIKE ME.   He's smart LIKE HER.

If necessary, change the capitalized pronouns to SE style.

1. Just between YOU and I, our teacher's a real zero.
2. John and HER went to the zoo with Pete and I.
3. ME and HIM went to the movie with John and HER.

(continued)

4. Dan and HIM are tall like Michael and THEM.

5. It was ME who called HIM and you last night.

6. WE're as big and as strong as THEM.

7. The boss yells at Chitra and I all the time.

8. Do you and HIM want to walk to school with Sam and I?

9. Ami and HIM traveled through New England with Ed and I.

10. Send applications to HIM and I, but it's ME who really wants the job.

11. HER and HIM can help YOU and I do our homework.

12. US guys are stronger than THEM.

13. ME and my brother saw that Bulls game with SHE and her sister.

14. It's ME who needs the help, not HIM.

15. All of my friends registered for Math with Susie and I.

Which rule applies to the capitalized SE pronouns?

1. WE'll keep this little secret just between YOU and ME.

2. HE and I always go to the movies with Tom and HER.

3. Do THEY want to go shopping with Cynthia and ME?

4. It's I who always cleans up for HER and HIM.

5. It's SHE who sometimes calls HER and HIM too late at night.

6. THEY are hungrier than WE.

7. SHE is strong like HIM.

8. WE are as smart as THEY.

9. SHE and I went to the concert with Leon and HIM.

10. THEY send cards to HIM and ME every year.

GO Find the COPula Again (Use of be-verbs)

When SE speakers use IS and ARE as sentence connectors, they are called COPULAS (see page 88). ARE is the copula in the sentence, "There ARE my friends." American BE dialect allows the use of GO as a copula after the words THERE and HERE, as in the contrasting sentence, "There GO my house."

Study the following sentence-pairs to determine if you use the SE be-verb copula and/or the GO copula. Accustom yourself to the SE style of using IS and ARE, before going on to the practice sentences.

GO COPULA	IS-ARE COPULA
There go my old house.	There's my old house.
Here go my mom, now.	Here's my mom, now.
There go my new friends.	There are my new friends.
There go Len in that Ford.	There's Len in that Ford.
Here go all my new books.	Here are all my new books.
There go Mia on the corner.	There's Mia on the corner.

Answer the following questions using SE copulas. If you are not sure about which be-verb to use, just repeat the one that the question uses.

1. Where's your old house? (There's/Here's my old house.)

2. Where's your mom?

3. Where are your new friends?

4. Where's Len?

5. Where are all those new books that you bought?

6. Where's Mia supposed to be waiting?

7. Where's your new puppy?

8. Where are Dan and Ami?

9. Where's the new gymnastics coach?

10. Where's your red ski sweater?

11. Where are they?

12. Where is she?

Where's the Action? CAREFUL or CAREFULLY

Which sentence sounds more like your style? She drives CAREFUL. She drives CAREFULLY.

If you chose the first sentence, you are demonstrating a common grammatical feature that differs from SE: substitution of adjective CAREFUL for adverb CAREFULLY.

ADVERBS DESCRIBE the ACTION verb of the sentence; they usually END in -LY, and COME AFTER the VERBS they describe. Adjectives describe persons, places and things; they either come before the nouns they describe, or after be-verbs.

ADJECTIVES	ADVERBS
He has a STYLISH wardrobe.	He dresses STYLISHLY.
He has QUICK movements.	He moves QUICKLY.
She sings a JOYFUL song.	She sings JOYFULLY.
Her writing is BEAUTIFUL.	She writes BEAUTIFULLY.
He does GOOD work.	He works WELL.

Read the following sentence-pairs until you feel comfortable describing action with -LY words, in the SE style.

DIFFERENCE	SE
She smiles PRETTY.	She smiles PRETTILY.
He talks BOASTFUL.	He talks BOASTFULLY.
He acts INTELLIGENT.	He acts INTELLIGENTLY.
I walk SLOW.	I walk SLOWLY.
I write CLEAR.	I write CLEARLY.

Change the following capitalized adjectives to SE adverbs.

1. She dresses so STYLISH and EXPENSIVE.
2. My mom talks too FAST and too SOFT.
3. She speaks INTELLIGENT but acts HYSTERICAL.
4. Slice the rolls CAREFUL or you'll hurt yourself BAD.
5. He wants me to act AFFECTIONATE and INTIMATE.
6. That teacher doesn't grade FAIR and she smiles PHONY.
7. I have to talk PERFECT and GRAMMATIC for my dad.
8. My dog barks LOUD, drinks SLOPPY and bites GENTLE.

No IFs or WHENs About It!

SE speakers use words called conjunctions to connect mini-sentences (clauses) within a sentence. "She asked IF she could leave WHEN Dan does" illustrates the use of two common SE conjunctions, IF and WHEN. Differences occur when conjunctions are omitted, or if vocabulary and word order differ. Which of the sentence-pairs is your style?

DIFFERENCE	SE
We don't know can he go.	We don't know IF he can go.
She asked could she leave.	She asked IF she could leave.
I asked did he mean it.	I asked IF he meant it.
Iffen he can, he will go.	IF he can, he will go.
Even he's tired, he works.	EVEN IF he's tired, he works.
We wondered did he stay.	We wondered IF he stayed.
Dan asked were we tired.	Dan asked IF we were tired.
Time we come, he'll leave.	WHEN we come, he'll leave.
Time we arrived it was over.	BY THE TIME we arrived....
I asked is it cold?	I asked IF it's cold.

Change the following sentences into SE style.

1. She asked can he go with her to the dance.

2. He asked did he need a tuxedo.

3. She said iffen he wants to he can wear a tux.

4. He wondered did she like men in tuxedos.

5. She said time he wears it she'll like it.

6. He asked did she buy a formal dress.

7. She said time they go he'll find out.

8. He said iffen she wears one he'll be glad.

9. He asked did she like carnations or gardenias.

10. She asked can he bring a gardenia.

11. He asked did she want a limosine.

12. She said, "If you want one, I'll rent it."

13. He asked can she stay out late.

14. She said that if he wanted to she'd stay out late.

WHO's on 1st? WHICH, WHAT, or THAT

Some clauses (mini-sentences) in SE begin with the pronouns WHO, WHICH, WHAT, or THAT: "She is the one WHO TAUGHT THE CLASS." Some English dialects use these clauses, but they may use different pronouns, and/or they may omit the pronouns. For example, some speakers use WHAT instead of the Standard English WHO, and/or do not use a pronoun in the clause. Study the following sentence-pairs so that you can identify the differences, and determine which examples characterize your speaking style.

SE	She's the lady WHO sold me the car.
Diff.	She's the lady WHAT sold me the car.
SE	I had a dog THAT was hit by a bus.
Diff.	I had a dog was hit by a bus.
SE	The books WHICH he moved are there.
Diff.	The books WHAT he moved are there.
SE	He owns a house THAT looks like a palace.
Diff.	He owns a house WHICH IT looks like a palace.

Change the capitalized pronouns to SE style and/or add SE pronouns.

1. There's the man WHAT told me about you.

2. I see the customer WHAT bought so much.

3. That's the horse was ridden by Shoemaker.

4. There was once an old woman lived in a shoe.

5. I owned a car WHICH IT purred like a cat.

6. Jamie is the friend WHAT calls me every night.

7. I bought a radio WHICH IT doesn't work now.

8. I'm so mad I could scream.

9. Are we sure she's the one WHAT borrowed my tools?

10. She bakes an apple pie tastes like nectar.

11. Dan's the player WHAT calls all the signals.

12. Ami's the girl WHAT has the curly hair.

WHO or WHOM?

WHO is a DOER; it does the action, or comes after a be-verb; WHOM is a DOEE; the action of the verb is done to it, or it comes after a preposition. They are usually the subjects and objects of their own mini-sentences (clauses). They always REFER TO PEOPLE, NOT THINGS. (Refer to page 118.) The WHO and WHOM clauses in the following sentences are capitalized to emphasize how they act as clause-subjects and objects.

SENTENCE	CLAUSE
He is the candidate WHOM WE LIKE.	(We LIKE WHOM)
She is the woman WHO WON THE BET.	(WHO WON the bet)
I'm the one WHO CALLED YOU.	(WHO CALLED you)
I'm the one WHOM YOU CALLED.	(You CALLED WHOM)
WHO IS THIS?	(This IS WHO?)
Is he the one TO WHOM YOU GAVE THE TIE?	(TO WHOM?)
WITH WHOM am I speaking?	(WITH WHOM?)
He's the one FOR WHOM I VOTED.	(FOR WHOM)
You are the character ABOUT WHOM I WROTE.	(ABOUT WHOM)
WHO ARE THE WINNERS?	(The winners ARE WHO?)

Study the following sentence-pairs. Note that in SE, you do not end a sentence with a preposition. You are also more likely to use the SE form of WHOM if you remember to put it after the preposition.

DIFFERENCE	SE
Who're you talking to?	TO WHOM are you talking?
Who're you rooming with?	WITH WHOM are you rooming?
Who're you voting for?	FOR WHOM are you voting?
Who're you playing against?	AGAINST WHOM are you playing?
Who's he writing it about?	ABOUT WHOM is he writing it?
Who's she standing between?	BETWEEN WHOM is she standing?

Fill in the blanks with WHO, WHOM and SE prepositions.

1. He's the one _____ hired me.

2. He's the one _____ I hired.

3. She's the salesperson _____ sold you the coat.

(continued)

4. She's the one _____ _____ I sold the coat.

5. _____ _____ am I speaking?

6. _____'s running against you in the race?

7. _____ _____ are you running in the race?

8. _____'s talking, please?

9. There's the baby _____ _____ I babysat.

10. He's the man _____ I hit with my car.

11. Roger, _____ is my oldest friend, has moved to California.

12. Valorie, _____ I write once a week, has moved to North Carolina with her husband, _____ retired last year.

13. Linda, _____ _____ I roomed for two years, married a man _____ was my husband's best friend.

14. Tell me the name of the person _____ you admire the most.

15. Tell me the name of the person _____ is your role model.

16. Tell me the name of the person _____ _____ you are a role model.

17. Once in a while you have a teacher _____ you will remember for the rest of your life.

18. I bought some roses, but I still don't know _____ _____ I'm going to give them.

19. _____ wants to go for pizza with me?

20. I am the only student _____ the teacher criticizes.

Prepositions

Words that suggest position, direction, time and other abstract relationships are called prepositions. They connect nouns or pronouns with other words. TO is a preposition in the sentence, "I ran TO the store." TO connects I with STORE. Other English dialects, including American BE, sometimes differ from SE regarding the use of prepositions. They might differ in their word choices and/or not need to use a preposition in a particular kind of phrase. Study the following sentence-pairs to determine which prepositional style you use most of the time.

SE	DIFFERENCE
Get out OF this house now.	Get out this house now.
Knit it out OF wool.	Knit it outta wool.
She's over AT Jan's house.	She's over Jan's house.
Let's go over TO Sarah's.	Let's go over by Sarah's.
Get out OF the car here.	Get out the car here.
Walk out OF this room.	Walk out this room.
He works AT that store.	He works that store.
I'm going TO the library.	I'm going by the library.
Let's get out OF here.	Let's get outta here.

Change the following sentences into SE sentences.

1. Let's get outta here before it's too late.

2. Jake is over by Grandpa's house.

3. She got out the car at the stop light.

4. He ran out the house, and then he saw her.

5. Ami jumped out the car and ran home.

6. Celia went by school to get the books she needed.

7. Mom is making my prom dress outta silk.

8. How can you walk out this room just like that?

9. Is Edward over by Marty's or over by Les'?

10. Take me by Jill's house so I can bring a toy to Jake.

"SALLY FORTH"

Sally Forth keeps interrupting Hilary's story because she wants her daughter to use oral SE grammar. Fill in each of the empty "bubbles" with SE grammatical features BEFORE you look at the next square, which tells you if you and the mother agree.

If you were not able to give the SE features for each of Hilary's remarks, refer to the appropriate lessons for more practice.

Square 1. - Pages 76, 106
Square 2. - Pages 112, 89
Square 3. - Page 116
Square 4. - Page 78
Square 5. - Pages 95, 78

Final Practice Exam for SE Grammar

Read the following story aloud into a tape recorder. Try to identify the grammatical features that differ from SE grammar and replace them with the SE alternatives. Reviewing the tape will help you identify additional features that need practice.

Beth and Althea been shopping for they summer wardrobes. They was tired and thirsty. They notice an air-condition restaurant where they been at several times. A waiter come to the table, and Beth say, "We tired and thirsty! We have drank some delicious sodas here, but your menu don't list them no more." The waiter goes, "Turn the page, and you-ah see them," and Beth goes, "Where they at?" Althea goes, "Here they are, Beth!" as she points to the list of the restaurant's drinks.

Althea said, "I've come here many times. I know exactly what's on the menu, and exactly what I want." The waiter nodded and said, "I seen you before, Miss, but I ain't seen her," pointing to Beth. "I be coming here almost every night," Beth exclaimed. "I be workin' days," the waiter said. Althea said, "I've eaten the 'Easy-On-The-Lips-Years-On-The-Hips-Banana-Split' so I'll have the 'Run-Three-Miles-Later-Sundae'." "Excellent choice," said the waiter, adding, "And you, Miss?" Beth said, "I gon have the 'Pile-High-With-Fudge-and-10-Scoop-of-Ice-Cream'." The waiter asked can he get them orders real quick now and Beth said, "Time you get 'em, we-ah be starving!" Just then, Althea and Beth heard a familiar voice saying, "Where you two been at – you ain't around at all no more." "There go Mel and Len," Beth yelled, adding, "it's a lot of old friends be comin' here all the time, but we don't never see you two." Len was noticeable quiet. Finally, he say to Althea, "I've began a letter to you five time, and five time I've tore it up." Althea glared and snarled back, "Well, I've begun ten letters, I've written ten letters, and I haven't torn any up. I've mailed all of them and have never gotten any from you." "There's a lotta reasons for that," said Len, adding, "Why don't you and her come with Mel and I, and we-ah go somewhere else. It's a place down the block where they make ice cream theirselves." "Here come our waiter, now," said Beth to Len and Mel, "and time you out the door we be done forgot about you!" Len said, "You the ones what call to us – you ain't who we wanna be with. Them girls over there, they the ones. Later!"

SECTION III: APPENDICES

APPENDIX A: Answers to Drills

Page 32. The necessary SE third person singular present tense changes to the paragraph are:

> "My boss LOVES it when she KNOWS I've made a mistake. She TELLS me that I'm a good worker but she CORRECTS me all the time. For instance, when she first COMES into the office and LOOKS at me, she SAYS, 'Good morning, Mary.' But then she always SAYS, 'Please get off of the phone, now.' Then, when she CHECKS my work she usually SAYS, 'This letter LOOKS pretty good, Mary, but it DOES need retyping.' Sometimes, she CALLS me into her office and ASKS me to get some coffee. That only BOTHERS me if I'm busy retyping the letter."

The necessary changes to the sentences are:

1. scares, makes   2. talks, gets   3. goes, rings   4. seems, goes   5. lives
6. brushes   7. misses, goes   8. reads, goes

Page 79. The following is a list of words from the Final Practice Pronunciation Exam. The featured sounds are capitalized and their respective page references are listed for additional practice. Repeated words are listed only once.

Paragraph 1

WORDS	PAGES	WORDS	PAGES
AFTER	64, 65, 3, 41	stoPPED	4, 12
BeTH	46, 22	THe	22
AND	64, 65, 3	FIRST	52, 41, 3
ALTHeA	8, 23, 66	aIR	41
WENT	51, 59, 4	cOndITIONED	66, 63, 50, 3
SHoppING	50, 38, 40	reSTAUraNT	3, 66, 4
THey	22, 20	notICED	63, 3, 12

(continued)

WORDS	PAGES
ASKED	10
WaiTER	51, 47, 41
WhAT'S	51, 66, 5
BeST	46, 3
Ice	61
CoLD	8
ON	62, 59, 78
THIs	22, 63
lIST	63, 3
THE	22, 72
smILED	61, 54, 8, 12
suGGesTED	18, 12
A	72, 75
STRAINED	15, 65, 3, 12
FRUit	74
hEALTHY	55, 8, 23, 63
reFreSHING	52, 50, 38, 40

WORDS	PAGES
WATCHED	51, 62, 50, 12
WhILE	51, 56, 36
AnOTHER	66, 22, 41
CUSTOmER	20, 69, 3, 41
PICKED	52, 63, 4, 12
sOmeTHING	69, 23, 38, 40
FINISHED	52, 63, 50, 12
IT	63, 47
THAT	22, 64, 47
SHe	50
POInTED	52, 61, 12
tO	72
cUSTOmER'S	66, 3, 41, 26
DrINK	47, 59
THaT'S	22, 5
mASHED	64, 50, 12
JUIce	49, 71

Paragraph 2

WORDS	PAGES
grASPED	64, 4, 12
mENu	59, 40
GaZED	20, 65, 26, 12
DOWN	47, 61, 40
BEEN	46, 59, 78
stUDyING	69, 47, 38
whoLe	36
AN	72, 75
EXTRA	18, 15
PILED	52, 61, 56, 8, 12
hIGH	61
FUDGE	52, 69, 49
WITH	51, 63, 23
tEN	59, 40
kINDS	61, 26, 28
oF	52, 77, 20
IceS	61, 26, 28

WORDS	PAGES
toLD	8
hER	41
IT'S	59, 5, 75
OUR	61, 41
moST	3
FOR	52, 62, 41
IteM	61, 40
hER	41
EYES	61, 26, 28
glAZED	65, 26, 12
rISKED	63, 5, 12
GAInING	20, 65, 38, 40
BACK	46, 64, 45
ALL	62, 57, 36
pOUNDS	61, 3, 26
lOST	62, 3
ONe	51, 69, 40
nUTS	69, 5

Paragraph 3

WORDS	PAGES	WORDS	PAGES
GASPED	20, 64, 4, 12	drINKS	59, 28
AT	64, 47	lISTS	63, 5
CHOIce	50, 61	YouR	49, 41
YOU	49, 71	PERhAPS	52, 41, 64, 27
mISS	63, 26	cAN	64, 40
lOOKING	71, 20, 38, 40	SHARe	50, 65, 41
lAUGHED	64, 52, 3, 12	lOOKED	71, 4, 12
THERE	22, 72, 41	STRAIghT	15, 65, 47
ARE	72, 41	YELLED	49, 55, 8, 12
JUST	72, 49, 3	WORST	51, 41, 3
mANY	59, 63	sALe	55, 36

Paragraph 4

WORDS	PAGES	WORDS	PAGES
THEN	22, 59, 40	cOmplAINED	66, 65, 3, 12
mEL	55, 36	sUCCess	69, 18
lEN	59, 40	cAN'T	65, 40, 4
gIRLS'	41, 8, 26, 27	dEcIDe	66, 61, 45
mALe	55, 36	BY	46, 61
FrIENdS	52, 59, 26, 27	THEMsELVeS	22, 59, 55, 28
FrOM	52, 69, 40	I'LL	61, 56, 36
schOOL	71, 36	hELP	55, 8
wAlKED	62, 4, 12	AnnOUNCED	66, 61, 40, 12
DOOR	47, 62, 41	SHE'LL	50, 54, 63, 36
THeiR	22, 41	pOIntING	61, 38, 40
oLD	8, 47	eXCEllENT	18, 66, 4
hAPPENING	65, 52, 38, 40	CHICAgo	77, 50, 62
AS	64, 26	FRUITY	74, 63
rEACHED	63, 50, 12	speCIAL	50, 66, 36
SHAKe	50, 65, 45	AdDED	64, 47, 12
hANdS	64, 3, 26	EXTRaORdinARily	18, 15, 62, 41, 44
JOInED	49, 61, 3, 12	ILLINOIS	54, 77, 61
THEM	22, 59, 40	crUSHED	69, 50, 12
YOU	49, 71	STRAWS	15, 62, 26, 28
ORdERING	62, 41, 38, 40	spOONS	71, 40, 26, 28
OR	62, 41	bIBS	63, 46, 26, 28
crEAM	63, 40		

Paragragh 5

WORDS	PAGES	WORDS	PAGES
eXCIteDly	18, 61, 47	hIMSELF	59, 55, 8
ANYTHING	59, 23, 38, 40	I	61
AnswERED	41, 12	kIND oF	61, 3, 51, 77
tIRED	61, 12	FEEL	52, 54, 36
WE'Ve	51, 63, 45, 51	lIKe	61, 45
eXERcISED	18, 41, 61, 26, 12	FILL	52, 54, 36
hOURS	61, 41, 26, 28	CHILLED	50, 54, 8, 12
TODAY	72, 47	lIMe	61, 40
DoN'T	47, 4	THINGS	23, 38, 40, 26
waNT	4	sAMe	65, 40
WILL	51, 54, 36	hAVING	64, 51, 38
HUNDRED	77, 47	PERFeCT	52, 41, 4
FIFTY	76, 3	CHOIcES	50, 61, 26, 28
FRUITS	74, 71, 5	sePTEMbER	4, 77, 59, 41
hE'LL	54, 63, 36	ENJOY	59, 49, 61

Page 82. The SE changes to the double-negative sentences are:

1. anything 2. anywhere 3. ever, anybody 4. any 5. ever, anything 6. a
7. anything, anyone 8. ever, anything 9. any 10. any

Page 83. The single negative SE answers to the questions are:

1. No, I don't have ANY... 2. No, I'm not doing ANYTHING... 3. No, I'm
not going ANYWHERE... 4. No, I don't know ANYBODY... 5. No, I don't
like lamb chops. 6. No, I don't want ANY... 7. No, this radio NEVER works.
(or) No, ...doesn't EVER work. 8. No, I don't have A dog.
9. No, I won't give you A watch... 10. No, I've not (I haven't) received ANY
parking tickets.

Page 84. The SE answers to the "ain't" questions are:

1. No, I HAVEN'T... 2. No, he ISN'T... 3. No, Sally'S NOT...(or) Sally ISN'T... 4. No, that car ISN'T (or) that car'S NOT... 5. No, her name ISN'T Mary. 6. No, he'S NOT... 7. No, we'RE NOT (or) we AREN'T finished. 8. No, those pictures AREN'T pretty.

The SE alternatives to the "ain't" sentences are:

1. isn't 2. isn't, isn't either 3. isn't, isn't 4. isn't, any 5. isn't, a 6. aren't, any 7. haven't, ever, anywhere 8. aren't 9. aren't 10. haven't (or) have never 11. isn't 12. There isn't any (or) There's not any 13. There isn't any 14. There's no 15. There isn't a

Page 86. The -ING and be-verbs are:

1. are going 2. are going 3. are trying 4. 'm sleeping 5. 're going

The SE changes are:

1. 's paying, 's not treating 2. 's reading, 's not sleeping 3. 's mowing, is planting 4. 're getting 5. 're wondering, 're ever going 6. is thinking 7. 's talking 8. 's working 9. 're going 10. 's cooking, 's baking 11. 're going 12. 's trying 13. 's too tired 14. 're happy 15. Are you

Page 88. The copulas in the sentences are:

1.'re, 's 2. 's, 's 3. are 4. 's, 's 5. are 6. are 7. 's, 8. are 9. are, 're 10. 're, 're

Page 90. The SE present and past tense be-verbs are:

1. My mom IS (WAS) 2. She IS (WAS) 3. My dad IS (WAS) 4. He IS (WAS) 5. My sister IS (WAS), My sisters ARE (WERE) 6. She IS (WAS), or, They ARE (WERE) 7. My brother IS (WAS), or, My brothers ARE (WERE) 8. He IS (WAS), or, They ARE (WERE) 9. My cousins ARE (WERE) 10. My aunt IS (WAS) 11. My uncle IS (WAS)

(continued)

1. President Kennedy IS (WAS) 2. Mayor Washington IS (WAS) 3. The kids of today ARE (WERE) 4. My friends and I ARE (WERE) 5. I AM (WAS)
6. My classmates ARE (WERE) 7. You and the others ARE (WERE)
8. Chicago IS (WAS)

Page 91. The necessary SE changes for WAS and WERE are:

1. Were 2. weren't 3. - 4. Were, were 5. were 6. - , were 7. were
8. - , - 9. Were 10. - , were 11. were 12. were 13. were 14. - 15. were
16. were 17. - 18. were 19. weren't 20. -

Page 92. The SE changes to the repetitive action "be" sentences are:

1. I'm always (I always am) tired 2. ...what he does 3. Tom always makes...
4. Sometimes we have fun ... we're bored. 5. They go... 6. My baby cries...
7. ...it's just (it just is) that way sometimes. 8. He's so sad... 9. We talk and
laugh... 10. Caroline gets... 11. ...never are open... 12. He never watches...

Page 93. The SE changes to the future "be" sentences are:

1. He'll (He will) see (or) He'll be seeing you... 2. Where will you be...
3. I'll be waiting (or) I'll wait... 4. Dan'll be... 5. Ami will get... 6. Linda
will wait..., when she's finished... 7. He'll never call if he's... 8. We always
go... 9. David will graduate... 10. Life will be...

Page 95. The SE changes to the capitalized verbs are:

1. says 2. has 3. - 4. doesn't 5. Does 6. - 7. doesn't 8. says 9. says, has
10. has 11. don't 12. have 13. - 14. - 15. doesn't 16. says, - , -

Page 96. The SE changes to the capitalized verbs in the story are:

1. says 2. doesn't 3. doesn't 4. say, has 5. says, has, doesn't 6. say, don't,
does, doesn't, goes

Page 97. The SE changes to the capitalized verbs are:

1. - 2. He's been 3. - 4. - 5. - 6. - 7. We've been 8. - 9. has not been
10. Jenny's been 11. We've been 12. have been

Page 100. The necessary SE changes to the "Where ... at?" sentences are:

1. Where are we? 2. Where's the party? 3. Where are they? 4. -
5. ...know where your man is. 6. Do you know where your teenager is?
7. - 8. Where's the el stop? 9. ...wherever he is. 10. ...where your house keys are? 11. -

Page 101. The necessary SE changes to the sentences are:

1. There's a... 2. There're (There are) so many... 3. There are... 4. - 5. There are a lot... 6. There's a sweater... 7. There're 8. - 9. There's a lot...

Page 102. The answers to the SE questions begin with:

1. There are... 2. There is... 3. There are... 4. There are... 5. There are...
6. There's a... 7. There's a... 8. There are...

Page 103. The SE changes to the two stories are:

1. ... my friend says ... My friend's name is ... Mary thinks ... My mom thinks ... but my dad thinks ...

2. That man ... is Mr. Smith ... Mr. Smith is ... Jane and I think ... The two of us pretend ... And General just salutes ...

3. That woman ... Mrs. Feller ... My son ... Mrs. Feller ... My son ... His teacher .... His bedroom ...

Page 104 and 105. The SE changes to the sentences are:

1. You have to go ... I have a lot... 2. He has to clean ... we have company...
3. Sandy has lots... 4. Ben has to balance... 5. - ,...but she has to get ... she has a house... 6. I have to get... 7. ...I have to... 8. Dan has an... 9. They have to... or I have... 10. I have to say ... you have a lot...

Page 109. The SE verb forms are:

1. done, did 2. came, come 3. drank, drunk 4. wrote, written 5. saw, seen
6. swam, swum 7. taken, took 8. rang, rung 9. ran, run 10. went, gone
11. threw, thrown 12. spoke, spoken 13. began, begun

Page 111. The necessary SE changes to the sentences are:

1. ...those potholes. 2. Those tires... 3. Those books... 4. ...those kids...
5. ...those invoices... 6. ...those Bulls? 7. ...those dogs... 8. those other...
9. ...those sweaters? 10. Those... 11. ...those reports... 12. Those guys...

Page 113. The SE changes to the capitalized pronouns are:

1. ...between you and ME... 2. John and SHE went...with PETE and ME
3. HE and I went with John and HER... 4. Dan and HE are...like Michael and THEM. 5. It was I... who called HIM 6. ...as THEY, - ... 7. ...at Chitra and ME... 8. Do you and HE want...with Sam and ME? 9. Ami and HE traveled...with Ed and ME. 10. to HIM and ME...It's I... 11. SHE and HE...YOU and ME 12. WE...than THEY. 13. My brother and I...with her sister and HER. 14. It's I...not HE. 15. ...with Susie and ME.

Page 115. The SE answers are:

1. There's 2. There's 3. There are 4. There's 5. There are 6. There's where
7. Here's 8. Here are 9. Here's 10. Here's 11. They're here. 12. There she is.

Page 116. The SE changes are:

1. stylishly, expensively 2. too quickly and softly 3. intelligently, hysterically 4. carefully, badly 5. affectionately and intimately 6. fairly, phonily 7. perfectly and grammatically 8. loudly, sloppily, gently.

Page 117. The SE changes are:

1. She asked IF HE COULD GO...   2. He asked IF HE NEEDED...
3. She said THAT IF he wants...   4. He wondered IF SHE LIKES
5. She said THAT BY THE TIME...   6. He asked IF SHE BOUGHT...
7. She said THAT WHEN...   8. He said THAT IF...   9. He asked IF SHE
LIKED...   10. She asked IF HE WOULD...   11. He asked IF SHE
WANTED...   12. -   13. ...IF SHE COULD...   14. -

Page 118. The SE changes are:

1. ...the man WHO...   2. ...the customer WHO...   3. ...the horse WHICH...
4. ...a woman WHO   5. ...a car THAT purred...   6. the friend WHO...
7. ...a radio THAT doesn't...   8. ...mad THAT...   9. ...the one WHO...
10. ...an apple pie THAT...   11. ...the player WHO...   12. ...the girl WHO...

Page 119. The SE answers are:

1. who 2. whom 3. who 4. to whom 5. With whom 6. Who's
7. Against whom 8. Who's 9. for whom 10. whom   11. who   12. whom, who
13. with whom, who   14. whom   15. who   16. for whom   17. whom   18. to
whom   19. Who   20. whom

Page 121. The SE changes are:

1. Let's get OUT OF here. 2. Jake is OVER AT Grandpa's house. 3. She got
OUT OF the car... 4. He ran OUT OF the house... 5. Ami junped OUT OF the
window... 6. Celia went TO or INTO school... 7. Mom is making my prom
dress OUT OF silk. 8. How can you walk OUT OF this room... 9. Is Edward
OVER AT Marty's or OVER AT Les'. 10. Take me TO Jill's house...

Page 123. The columns on the following three pages contain grammatical features
from the Final Grammatical Practice Exam paragraphs, their necessary SE changes,
and their respective page references.

(continued)

Paragraph 1

GRAMMATICAL FEATURES	SE CHANGES	PAGES
been shopping	have been shopping	97, 106
they summer wardrobes	their summer wardrobes	98
They was	They were	89
notice	noticed	12
air-condition	air-conditioned	12
where they been at	where they've been	100, 97
A waiter come	A waiter comes	30, 95
Beth say	Beth says	30, 95
We have drank	We have drunk	106
We tired	We're tired	88, 89
your menu don't	your menu doesn't	95
no more	any more	82
The waiter goes	The waiter says	30, 78, 95
you-ah see them	you'll see them	94
and Beth goes	Beth says	30, 78, 95
Where they at?	Where are they?	100, 88
and Althea goes	Althea says	30, 78, 95
Here they are	-	115, 89
she points	-	30, 95
restaurant's drinks	-	29, 28

Paragraph 2

Althea said	-	78
I've come	-	106
many times	-	28
I know	-	95
exactly	-	116
I want	-	95
nodded, said	-	12, 78
I seen	I've seen	106
I ain't seen	I haven't seen	84, 106
I be coming	I come	92
Beth exclaimed	-	12

GRAMMATICAL FEATURES	SE CHANGES	PAGES
I be working	I work	92
the waiter said	-	78
I've eaten	-	106
I'll have	-	94
I gon have	I'm going to have	110
Pile-High	Piled-High	12
10-Scoop	10-Scoops	28
asked can he	asked if he could	117
them orders	those orders	111
quick	quickly	116
Time you	By the time you	117
get 'em	- them	111
we-ah be starving	we'll be starving	94

Paragraph 3

heard	-	106
Where ... at	Where...	100
you two been	have you been	97
you ain't	you aren't	84, 89
no more	any more	82
There go	There're	115, 101
it's a lot	There are a lot	101
be comin'	who come	92
we don't never	- ever	82
Len was	-	89
noticeable	noticeably	116
he say	he says	30, 95
I've began	I've begun	106
five time	five times	28
I've tore	I've torn	106
Althea glared, snarled	-	12
I've begun	-	106
ten letters	-	28
I've written	-	106

(continued)

GRAMMATICAL FEATURES	SE CHANGES	PAGES
I haven't torn any	-	106, 82
I've mailed	-	106, 12
(I)...have never gotten	-	106
any	-	82
There's a lotta	There are a lot of	101
Why don't you	-	95
(you) and her	you and she	112
with Mel and I	with Mel and me	112
we-ah go	we'll go	94
it's a place	there's a place	101
they make	-	95
theirselves	themselves	98
Here come	Here comes	30, 95
he got	he has	95, 104
hisself	himself	98, 77
time	by the time	117
you out the door	you're out of...	121
we be done forgot	we'll have forgotten	94, 106
You the ones	You're the ones	88, 89
the ones what	the ones who	118
call to us	called to us	12
you ain't	you aren't	84, 89
who...with	with whom	119
wanna be	want to be	76
them girls	those girls	111
them girls ... they	those girls are	111, 103
they the ones	they're the ones	88, 89

APPENDIX B: Broadcast Copy for Pronunciation Practice

This appendix presents copy samples of news, sports, weather, commercials, and public service announcements (PSAs). The best way to practice this copy is to do so after you have completed the drills and practice sentences for a particular SE feature. The following procedure for practicing Broadcast Copy is recommended:

1. READ the paragraph of copy SILENTLY to acquaint yourself with the content, consonants and vowels.

2. HIGHLIGHT or underline all the vowels, consonants and vowel-consonant combinations that you have just learned and practiced. For example, let's say you have completed all the pages on Consonant Clusters and -ED Word Endings. In the first paragraph of copy, you read "...A BAND OF MASKED MEN WHO HAD SERVED...STAGED AN UNSUCCESSFUL ATTEMPT..." You should underline (nd) in BAND, SKED (skt) in MASKED, RVED (rvd) in SERVED, GED (jd) in STAGED, and (mpt) in ATTEMPT as examples of consonant clusters.

3. Read the underlined or highlighted words as a DRILL until your SE production of these words is comfortable and effortless.

4. Finally, READ the COPY OUT LOUD into a tape recorder so you can hear your SE productions and/or any differences in pronunciation.

5. You can use the same paragraphs of copy over and over as you continue to master new SE features.

News Copy

#1 AUTHORITIES IN MANILA SAY THAT A BAND OF MASKED MEN, WHO HAD SERVED UNDER OUSTED PHILIPPINE RULER FERDINAND MARCOS, STAGED AN UNSUCCESSFUL ATTEMPT SATURDAY MORNING TO FREE A MARCOS ALLY WHO WAS JAILED ON MURDER CHARGES.

#2 A NEW CRACKDOWN ON GANG VIOLENCE IN LOS ANGELES IS TO CONTINUE AT LEAST THROUGH SATURDAY NIGHT. ABOUT ONE-THOU-SAND OFFICERS ARE BEING DEPLOYED IN NEIGHBORHOODS PLAGUED BY GANGS. IT'S THE BIGGEST SWEEP OF ITS KIND SINCE APRIL.

#3 A SECOND EARTHQUAKE HAS HIT SOUTHERN CALIFORNIA IN AS MANY DAYS. A MODERATE QUAKE THAT MEASURED FIVE-POINT-TWO

ON THE RICHTER SCALE HIT THE REGION FRIDAY AFTERNOON. ON THURSDAY, A TREMOR MEASURING TWO-POINT-SIX SHOOK DOWNTOWN LOS ANGELES.

#4 POLICE CARRYING BILLY CLUBS CONFRONTED SOME 200 YOUTHS, FRIDAY NIGHT, IN NORTHERN NEW JERSEY. THE FLARE-UP FOLLOWED TWO NIGHTS OF VIOLENCE IN PERTH AMBOY, SPARKED BY AN OFF-DUTY OFFICER'S FATAL SHOOTING OF RONALDO MARTINEZ, A MEXICAN IMMIGRANT.

#5 A REPORT RELEASED TODAY SAYS A GROWING NUMBER OF CHILDREN AND ADOLESCENTS ARE NEEDLESSLY TREATED AT PROFITABLE HOSPITAL INPATIENT PSYCHIATRIC UNITS, WHILE SOME LOW-INCOME YOUTHS WHO NEED TREATMENT, ARE TURNED AWAY. THE REPORT, RELEASED BY THE CITIZENS COUNCIL ON MENTAL HEALTH, SAYS MANY OF THE YOUTHS COULD HAVE BEEN TREATED AS EFFECTIVELY THROUGH ALTERNATIVE OUTPATIENT PROGRAMS, BUT ARE INSTITUTIONALIZED BECAUSE INSURANCE COMPANIES PICK UP THE TAB.

#6 RESEARCHERS PREDICT THAT ADVANCES IN GENETIC ENGINEERING WILL PRODUCE SUPERIOR CROPS THAT WILL BE ABLE TO RESIST DISEASE, DROUGHT AND POISONS. ROBERT GOLDBERG, A PLANT MOLECULAR BIOLOGIST AT UCLA, EXPECTS THAT NEW INSIGHTS INTO DNA MANIPULATION, WILL PRODUCE GENETICALLY REDESIGNED FRUITS AND VEGETABLES IN THE NEXT FIVE YEARS. GOLDBERG'S PREDICTIONS ARE IN THE CURRENT ISSUE OF "SCIENCE," A MONTHLY JOURNAL.

#7 THE NATION'S DEBT-RIDDEN FARMERS WERE HANDED A DEFEAT TODAY BY THE SUPREME COURT. THE HIGH COURT RULED UNANIMOUSLY THAT A FARMER'S EXPERIENCE AND LABOR CANNOT BE CONSIDERED CAPITAL IN CHAPTER ELEVEN BANKRUPTCY PROCEEDINGS.

#8 IN HARLEM, NEW YORK, A KIDNAPPING SUSPECT IS IN POLICE CUSTODY. HE SURRENDERED SIX HOURS AFTER BARRICADING HIMSELF IN A HOSPITAL SUB-BASEMENT. THE SUSPECT – WHO WAS HANDCUFFED TO A HOSPITAL BED – BROKE FREE, OVERPOWERED A POLICEMAN AND TOOK TWO HOSTAGES WHOM HE LATER FREED.

#9 PAT ROBERTSON HAS AGREED TO PAY COURT COSTS IN HIS 35 MILLION DOLLAR LIBEL SUIT AGAINST FORMER CALIFORNIA REPRESENTATIVE, PETE MCCLOSKEY. THE DECISION ENDS THE VERBAL SKIRMISH OVER ROBERTSON'S MARINE CORPS RECORD DURING THE KOREAN WAR.

#10 DISGRACED TELEVISION EVANGELIST, JIMMY SWAGGART, HAS PROMISED HIS FOLLOWERS HE WILL TELL THEM THE WHOLE STORY "SOME DAY WHEN THE TIME IS RIGHT." SWAGGART SAYS THAT FOR EIGHT MONTHS PRIOR TO HIS CONFESSION OF MORAL FAILURE, HE KNEW HE WAS "LOSING IT."

Sports Copy

#1 PREAKNESS WINNER, "RISEN STAR," AND KENTUCKY DERBY CHAMPION, "WINNING COLORS," HEAD A FIELD OF SIX THREE-YEAR-OLDS FOR TODAY'S BELMONT STAKES IN NEW YORK. "WINNING COLORS" IS TRYING TO BECOME THE FIRST FILLY TO CAPTURE TWO LEGS OF THE TRIPLE CROWN.

#2 MIKE MODANO OF THE DETROIT AREA AND TREVOR LINDEN OF MEDICINE HAT, ALBERTA, ARE THE TWO MOST HIGHLY RATED PLAYERS FOR TODAY'S NATIONAL HOCKEY LEAGUE DRAFT IN MONTREAL. MINNESOTA AND VANCOUVER HAVE THE TOP TWO PICKS.

#3 ERNEST RILES SINGLED, DOUBLED AND DROVE HOME TWO RUNS IN HIS NATIONAL LEAGUE DEBUT FRIDAY NIGHT, PACING THE SAN FRANCISCO GIANTS TO A 9-6 VICTORY OVER THE CINCINNATI REDS. ACQUIRED WEDNESDAY FROM MILWAUKEE FOR JEFFREY LEONARD, RILES ALSO RECORDED 10 ASSISTS AT THIRD BASE. WILL CLARK CONTRIBUTED A THREE-RUN HOMER AND CANDY MALDONADO HAD A SOLO BLAST AS THE GIANTS BUILT A 9-0 CUSHION. THE REDS SCORED THEIR SIX RUNS IN THE EIGHTH, WHEN ERIC DAVIS AND BARRY LARKIN EACH SINGLED HOME TWO RUNS.

#4 EVERY CHICAGO CUB STARTER, INCLUDING WINNING PITCHER JEFF PICO, GOT A HIT IN THE CUBS' 7-3 ROUT OF THE ST. LOUIS CARDINALS LAST NIGHT IN BUSCH STADIUM. ROOKIE MARK GRACE LED THE 19-HIT ATTACK WITH FOUR HITS AND THREE R-B-I-s. RYNE SANDBERG GOT TWO HITS IN FOUR AT BATS.

#5. THE CHICAGO WHITE SOX ENDED TEDDY HIGUERA'S 23-INNING SCORELESS STREAK WITH A 1-0 WIN OVER THE MILWAUKEE BREWERS LAST NIGHT. GREG WALKER DROVE IN DARYL BOSTON IN THE TENTH INNING FOR THE GAME WINNER. BOSTON, PINCH RUNNING FOR HAROLD BAINES, STOLE SECOND BASE AND WENT TO THIRD ON AN ERROR. WALKER HIT THE NEXT PITCH INTO RIGHT FIELD TO SCORE BOSTON. HIGUERA GOT THE LOSS. SOX RELIEVER, BILL LONG, PITCHED THE TENTH INNING FOR THE WIN.

#6 LOREN ROBERTS, WHO IS WINLESS IN SEVEN YEARS ON THE PRO GOLF TOUR, HOLDS A ONE-SHOT LEAD AT THE HALFWAY MARK OF THE 700-THOUSAND DOLLAR WESTCHESTER CLASSIC IN NEW YORK.

#7 COURTNEY SIGLER AND STACEY PALLER HAD TWO R-B-I'S APIECE AS MOLINE DEFEATED MAINE SOUTH 6-1 FRIDAY NIGHT IN THE CHAMPIONSHIP GAME OF THE ILLINOIS HIGH SCHOOL ASSOCIATION GIRLS SOFTBALL TOURNAMENT. MARTINA WENDT, WHO FINISHED THE SEASON WITH A PERFECT 17-0 RECORD, ALLOWED SIX HITS IN SIX INNINGS, ONE EARNED RUN, GAVE UP NO WALKS AND STRUCK OUT FIVE. SHE WAS NAMED THE TOURNEY'S MOST VALUABLE PLAYER.

#8 MICHAEL JORDAN SCORED 43 POINTS, GRABBED 10 REBOUNDS AND DISHED OUT FIVE ASSISTS TO LEAD THE CHICAGO BULLS TO A DECISIVE 112-99 VICTORY OVER THE TWO-TIME DEFENDING WORLD CHAMPION DETROIT PISTONS - LAST NIGHT AT CHICAGO STADIUM - IN FRONT OF 18,676 ECSTATIC FANS.

Weather Copy

#1 IT'S GOING TO BE PARTLY CLOUDY IN THE CHICAGO AREA TO-NIGHT WITH A LOW IN THE 30'S. INCREASING CLOUDINESS ON WEDNESDAY WITH HIGHS IN THE 60'S NEAR THE LAKE, AND IN THE 50'S IN THE WESTERN SUBURBS. IT WILL BE MOSTLY CLOUDY WITH A CHANCE OF SHOWERS WEDNESDAY NIGHT - LOWS IN THE MID 30'S TO MID 40'S - BECOMING MOSTLY SUNNY THURSDAY WITH HIGHS OF 50 TO 55.

#2 SUNNY SKIES MIXING WITH CLOUDS WILL DEVELOP LATER TODAY. HIGHS WILL BE IN THE MID-80'S WITH SLIGHTLY COOLER READINGS LAKESIDE. IT WILL BE BREEZY AND WARMER TONIGHT WITH LOWS IN THE MID-60'S.

#3 TOMORROW WE'LL SEE A MIXTURE OF SUN AND CLOUDS ONCE AGAIN WITH POSSIBLY AN ISOLATED STORM LATE IN THE DAY. HIGHS WILL BE IN THE MID-80'S. THERE'S A SLIGHT RISK OF A STORM TONIGHT WITH LOWS IN THE 60'S.

#4 WISCONSIN WILL HAVE CLOUDS ACCUMULATING DURING THE DAY WITH HIGHS FROM THE UPPER 70'S TO THE MID-80'S. THERE'S A POSSIBILITY OF A SHOWER IN THE NORTHWEST REGION OF THE STATE TONIGHT WITH LOWS FROM 59 TO 67.

#5 CHICAGO METROPOLITAN COMMUTERS WILL FIND ROAD CONDITIONS TO BE DRY TODAY, THANKS TO A SLOW MOVING HIGH PRESSURE SYSTEM NEAR WASHINGTON, D.C. FOR THIS MORNING'S RUSH HOUR, THE AVERAGE TEMPERATURE WILL APPROACH 68 DEGREES.

Commercial Copy

#1 YOU'LL GET ONE DOLLAR IN YOUR POCKET FOR TRYING ONE OF OURS! SAVE BIG ON DELICIOUS HOT POCKETS OR LEAN POCKETS BY PICKING ANY OF OUR TEN TASTE-TEMPTING FLAVORS - LIKE HEARTY HAM 'N CHEESE OR PEPPERONI PIZZA. FOR ALL YOU CALORIE COUNTERS, TRY ZESTY CHICKEN PARMESAN LEAN POCKETS. IT'S THE TASTY HOT MEAL WITHOUT A BIG DEAL. HOT POCKETS AND LEAN POCKETS...THEY'RE MICROWAVABLE.

#2 COOKING MAY BE A LABOR OF LOVE, BUT WHO SAYS IT HAS TO BE LONG HOURS OF HARD LABOR? NOT MCCORMICK/SCHILLING. WE SAY - GIVE YOURSELF A BREAK AND PUT A DELICIOUS MEAL ON THE TABLE FOR YOUR FAMILY WITH OUR SEASONING MIXES. WHETHER IT'S SPAGHETTI, SLOPPY JOES OR TACOS, YOU'LL SEE THAT GREAT COOKING COMES FAST AND EASY WHEN YOU CUT CORNERS WITH MCCORMICK/ SCHILLING...THE HEART OF GREAT COOKING.

#3 IVORY LIQUID - THE RICH SUDS THAT LEAVE YOUR HANDS FEELING SOFT AND SMOOTH. BUY IVORY LIQUID AT YOUR GROCERY TODAY.

#4 COME INTO THE SEARS PORTRAIT STUDIO AND GET SEVEN FREE PORTRAITS WHEN YOU BUY OUR $14.95 PACKAGE. COME INTO THE SEARS PORTRAIT STUDIO THIS WEEK AND GET 16 ADDITIONAL MINI-PORTRAITS. THAT'S A TOTAL OF 23 PORTRAITS - A VALUE WORTH $58.85 FOR ONLY $14.95. A REMEMBERANCE THAT LASTS A LIFETIME IS WAITING FOR YOU AT THE SEARS PORTRAIT STUDIO.

#5 MIGHT I SUGGEST A PROPER HOT LUNCH? WHY SETTLE FOR A COLD MEATLOAF SANDWICH OR A CARTON OF YOGURT - WHEN YOU CAN HAVE A PROPER HOT LUNCH WITH LUNCH BUCKET MEALS. LUNCH BUCKET MICROWAVABLE MEALS COOK UP HOT AND DELICIOUS IN SECONDS. AND THEY COME IN SEVENTEEN DELECTABLE VARIETIES. EVERYTHING FROM BEEF STEW AND LASAGNA TO HALF A DOZEN DIFFERENT SOUPS. TAKE MY SUGGESTION - LUNCH BUCKET MICROWAVABLE MEALS.

#6 I'LL TAKE GOOD OLD-FASHIONED PIE ANY OLD DAY - AND I BET YOU WILL TOO. SO TAKE MRS. SMITH'S FULLY BAKED "PIE-IN-MINUTES" RIGHT OFF YOUR GROCER'S FREEZER'S SHELF. JUST POP IT IN THE OVEN, OR, INTO YOUR MICROWAVE, AND YOU'LL HAVE GOOD OLD-FASHIONED, SLOW-BAKED, DELICIOUSNESS, BEFORE YOU KNOW IT! MRS. SMITH'S "PIE-IN-MINUTES" - JUST LIKE MOM'S.

#7 EVERY DAY MORE AND MORE AMERICANS ARE TRYING TO CUT DOWN ON CHOLESTEROL AND SATURATED FAT. THAT'S WHY WE MAKE MOCHA MIX FOR YOU. MOCHA MIX - THE NON-DAIRY CREAMER WITH THE FRESH CREAMY TASTE. ENJOY DELICIOUS MOCHA MIX CREAMER IN YOUR COFFEE, IN CEREAL OR POURED OVER FRESH FRUIT. IT HAS NO CHOLESTEROL, IT'S LOW IN SATURATED FAT, AND IT'S 100 PER CENT MILK-FREE. LOOK FOR MOCHA MIX CREAMER IN YOUR GROCER'S DAIRY CASE TODAY. MOCHA MIX - A HEALTHIER ALTERNATIVE.

#8 COME TO THE KIDS STORE AT MONTGOMERY WARD, THE BRAND NAME SAVINGS STORE. ALL BOYS' TEES ON SALE - SIZES 4 THRU 20, FEATURING NINJA TURTLES TEES AND BART SIMPSON TEES ... AND ... ALL BOYS' JEANS ARE ON SALE WITH THE FEATURED SUPER BUY OF ONLY $10.99 FOR STONEWASHED JEANS - SIZES 8 THROUGH 14. ALL THIS AT THE BRAND NAME SAVINGS STORE - MONTGOMERY WARD.

#9 A CARNIVAL OF VALUES AT TRUE VALUE HARDWARE STORES. CHOOSE GREEN THUMB WASP & HORNET SPRAY FOR ONLY $1.88! AND, A FLEX-A-BIT EXTENSION KIT BY MASTER MECHANIC FOR ONLY $8.99! OR MAYBE YOU FEEL LIKE BRIGHTENING UP THE WALLS OF YOUR HOME WITH TRU-TEST E-Z KARE LATEX FLAT FINISH PAINT IN FLAT FINISH, FLAT ENAMEL, SEMI-GLOSS OR GLOSS - FROM ONLY $10.98 TO $19.98 A GALLON. YOU CAN'T BEAT THE VALUES AT TRUE VALUE.

#10 ZAP THOSE PESTY GNATS, WASPS AND BEES! A FLOWTRON 15-WATT ELECTRONIC INSECT KILLER CONTROLS PESTS IN AREAS UP TO 1/2 ACRE. ONLY $29.99 AT TRUE VALUE HARDWARE STORES.

#11 POST NATURAL BRAN FLAKES PROVIDES YOUR FAMILY WITH TWO-THIRDS MORE FIBER THAN THE LEADING OAT BRAN FLAKES. POST NATURAL BRAN FLAKES IS MADE WITH WHOLESOME WHEAT BRAN - A NATURAL SOURCE OF BULK IN YOUR DIET. IN FACT, WHEAT BRAN IS BETTER THAN OAT BRAN FOR KEEPING YOUR SYSTEM RUNNING SMOOTHLY. KEEPING YOU AT YOUR BEST - POST NATURAL BRAN FLAKES.

"PSA" (Public Service Announcement) Copy

#1 NEIGHBORS AGAINST DRUGS ASKS YOU TO HELP YOUR KIDS LEAD A DRUG-FREE LIFE. HELP THEM TO STAY HEALTHY AND HAPPY. HELP THEM TO HELP THEIR FRIENDS. HELP THEM TO STAND UP FOR WHAT THEY KNOW IS RIGHT. HELP THEM TO JUST SAY NO.

#2 LINCOLN SCHOOL PTA IS HAVING A RUMMAGE AND BAKE SALE, SATURDAY AND SUNDAY, OCTOBER 8TH AND 9TH, FROM 9 A.M. TO 6 P.M. IN THE LINCOLN SCHOOL GYMNASIUM. COME ENJOY DELICIOUS TREATS. FIND TERRIFIC BARGAINS. AND HELP PROVIDE LINCOLN SCHOOL CHILDREN WITH ART AND MUSIC PROGRAMS. THE LINCOLN SCHOOL BAKE AND RUMMAGE SALE - OCTOBER 8TH AND 9TH.

#3 IF SOMEONE IN YOUR FAMILY HAS A DRINKING PROBLEM, COME TO THE PEOPLE WHO CARE AND GIVE SOLUTIONS - ALYNON - WE'VE BEEN HELPING FAMILIES OF ALCOHOLICS FOR YEARS. NO GUILT - NO FIGHTS - JUST HELP. ALYNON.

#4 THE BLACK CAUCUS AT PARKWAY COLLEGE IS SPONSORING AN ART AND MUSIC FAIR. NO ENTRY FEE - JUST A SMALL DONATION WOULD BE APPRECIATED. BRING YOUR FAMILY AND FRIENDS - SUNDAY AT ONE P.M., NOVEMBER 10TH. WE'LL SEE YOU THERE!

#5 LAUREL SCHOOL KINDERGARTNERS ARE PRESENTING A THANKSGIVING PLAY ENTITLED, "THANK YOU FOR EVERYTHING". DON'T MISS THESE ENTERTAINING THESPIANS, WEDNESDAY, 7 P.M., NOV. 24TH.

APPENDIX C: Notes and Sources

As mentioned in the Introduction, the first "exhaustive and scholarly research" on the history of American Black Dialects was done by Lorenzo D. Turner, an African American linguist. His fifteen-year study of Gullah, an English dialect spoken by the inhabitants of coastal Georgia and South Carolina, revealed four thousand words and many rules of pronunciation and grammar that are derived from West African languages. For hundreds of years, many Americans were led to believe that the kidnapped African slaves had no culture, no rule-governed languages and no "real" history. This myth served as an excuse for slavery and racism. It is largely because of Turner's work that African Americans, like other Americans, can find part of their history in the very dialects they speak today. If you speak a variety of Black English, you might be interested in tracing the roots of some of your vocabulary, pronunciation and grammar in Lorenzo D. Turner's book, *Africanisms in the Gullah Dialect.*

Black English, by J.L. Dillard, various articles and research by William A. Stewart, and *Talkin and Testifyin*, by Geneva Smitherman, will also provide you with detailed, informative and entertaining facts about the origins, evolution and characteristics of Black English.

I found the Gaelic derivation of YOUSE, and the Scots-Irish derivation of Y'ALL, along with hundreds of other fascinating facts, in *The Story of English,* by Robert McCrum, William Cran, and Robert MacNeil. If you want to trace the origins of your own English dialect, or just want to read about the history of English and all its dialectic variations, this book and videoseries are highly recommended.

The philosophy and methodology of this manual, as well as specific descriptions of pronunciation and grammar, are based on the work of the authors acknowledged above, others who are listed in the Bibliography, and my own training, research and experience.

In the lessons, contrasting sentences and phrases present only one feature at a time, so that the reader can concentrate on acquiring one feature at a time. Authenticity, therefore, is sometimes sacrificed for simplicity and clarity. For example, the more realistic representation, "He be goin' firs errih day" is presented as "He be going first every day" so that only the Repetitive Action BE + ING is considered in that particular lesson.

The utilization of CONTRAST is a clinical and philosophical concept:

1. Speech therapists use a technique called NEGATIVE PRACTICE to encourage the student to practice the old as well as the new feature of speech. This helps to develop self-monitoring skills by bringing the old automatic style to the conscious awareness of the speaker. The method was originally used with people who had articulatory/stuttering/voice disorders, and/or with children who exhibited developmental speech problems. The term, Negative Practice, therefore, referred to a speech style that the speaker wanted to eliminate. It is for this reason that the manual refers to the technique as one of contrast and difference rather than "negative."

2. Ralph Ellison's remarks that are quoted in the beginning of the manual, reflect the philosophical view of this contrasting technique. He was one of the first to suggest that teachers help their sudents to become bi-dialectic.

SECTION IV: INTERNATIONAL PHONETIC ALPHABET (IPA)

The International Phonetic Alphabet is a set of pronunciation symbols. Each symbol represents the smallest unit of speech that can be differentiated from other individual speech sounds. The term, phoneme, refers to the individual speech sounds, and the IPA is the means by which these phonemes are displayed in print.

The IPA will help you learn to differentiate between letters and sounds. For example, if I asked you to spell "beat" out loud, you would probably begin by saying "bee", for the (b) sound. You will learn, however, that "bee" has two phonemes, (b) and "ee", and that you should produce (b) without a following vowel sound. Then, say "ee" for "ea", represented in the IPA by (i). End with a (t), without the "ee" following it. In IPA, therefore, you would say and write "beat" as (b) (i) (t).

Although experts compiled the IPA to represent the world's speech sounds, the following charts present only those symbols that represent the General American/ Broadcast style of pronouncing American English vowels and consonants. The charts also present: spellings that this text uses to cue pronunciation; sample words; and page numbers of related lessons. The "Dev. Age" column lists the ages after which children can be expected to learn the consonant sounds.

On the charts, PLACE refers to the two parts of the mouth that are used to produce a speech sound. For CONSONANTS: Bi-labial = two lips; Labio-dental = (bottom) lip under (top-front) teeth; Tip-dental = tongue-tip between teeth; Tip-alveolar = tongue-tip touches hard palate; Blade-alveolar = tongue-body touches palate; Blade-prepalatal = tongue-body touches front part of palate; Front-palatal and Central-palatal = tougue-front touches front or central part of palate; Back-velar = tongue-back touches soft (back) palate; Glottal = vocal cords open. For VOWELS and DIPHTHONGS: HIGH, MID or LOW refers to how high or low in the mouth cavity the FRONT, CENTRAL or BACK part of the tongue must be in order to produce a particular vowel or diphthong.

MANNER refers to how the air stream is released during consonant production: Stop = blocked and/or puffed; Fricative = sustained release through narrow opening;

(continued)

Affricate = stopped, then released; Glide = sustained; Lateral = over sides of the tongue; Nasal = through the nostrils of the nose.

VOICING refers to whether or not the vocal cords vibrate during the production of a speech sound: VOICED (V) = vocal cords vibrate and produce sound; VOICELESS (V̶) = vocal cords do not vibrate; they open only to release a stream of air.

IPA PHONEMIC CONSONANTS:

IPA-SE SYMBOLS		DEV. AGE	SAMPLE WORDS	PLACE, MANNER, VOICING V̶ = Voiceless; V = Voiced		SST PAGES
p	p	3	paper, up	Bi-labial, Stop	V̶	4,20,45,52
b	b	5	Bobby, rob	Bi-labial, Stop	V	13,20,45,46
ʍ	wh	3	which, whim	Bi-labial, Fricative	V̶	100,118
w	w	3	was, lower	Bi-labial, Glide	V	51
m	m	3	mommy, some	Bi-labial, Nasal	V	6,40
f	f	4	feet, beef	Labio-dental, Fricative	V̶	3,20,52
v	v	7	Vivian, of	Labio-dental, Fricative	V	13,20,46,51
θ	th	7	thumb, bath	Tip-dental, Fricative	V̶	20,22-25
ð	th	8	the, mother	Tip-dental, Fricative	V	20,22-25
t	t	6	top, pot	Tip-alveolar, Stop	V̶	3,20,45,47
d	d	5	dad, lady	Tip-alveolar, Stop	V	3,12,20,47
l, *ɫ	l	6	lily, *call	Tip-alveolar, Lateral	V	8,36,54-57
n	n	3	no, rain	Tip-alveolar, Nasal	V	3,18,40,59
s	s	7	see, ice	Blade-alveolar, Fricative	V̶	3,15,20,26
z	z	7	zip, easy	Blade-alveolar, Fricative	V	13,20,26-33
ʃ	sh	6	she, wash	Blade-prepalatal, Fricative	V̶	13,15,20,50
ʒ	zh	7	measure	Blade-prepalatal, Fricative	V	20,21
tʃ	ch	6	chip, rich	Blade-prepalatal, Affricate	V̶	13,20,50
dʒ	j	7	jet, badge	Blade-prepalatal, Affricate	V	13,18,20,49
j	y	5	you, rayon	Front-palatal, Glide	V	16,49
r	r	6	run, corral	Central-palatal, Glide	V	15,44
k	k	4	cat, rake	Back-velar, Stop	V̶	5,10,16,20
g	g	4	go, bag	Back-velar, Stop	V	16,18,20,45
ŋ	ng	5	singing	Back-velar, Nasal	V	38,40
h	h	3	has, ahead	Glottal, Fricative	V̶	95,106,119

*The production for final (ɫ) and (ɫ)+consonant is achieved when the tongue-tip makes minimum contact with the hard palate; it is sometimes called "dark l". The initial and medial "light l" production is different because it occurs when maximum contact is made between the tongue-tip and the hard palate.

IPA PHONEMIC VOWELS:

IPA-SE SYMBOLS		SAMPLE WORDS	PLACE	SST PAGES
i	ee	key, seal, believe, easy	High-Front	54,61,63
ɪ	ih	hit, pin, did, fiddle	High-Front	40,54,59,63,65
u	o͞o	sue, suit, who, too, stew, rule	High-Back	71
ʊ	o͝o	book, put, look, woof	High-Back	69,71
e	ay	say, hey, wake, raid, lake	Mid-Front	55,65
ɛ	eh	sell, melt, held, end, bet	Mid-Front	55,59,64,65
ɝ	ER	hurt, shirt, her, first	Mid-Central	41,44
ɚ	er	better, another, father	Mid-Central	41,44
ʌ	UH	but, up, stunt, love, hover	Mid-Central	69
ə	uh	America, upon, atom, Detroit	Mid-Central	66
o	oh	hope, low, Joe, oh, goat, nose	Mid-Back	61
æ	ā	hat, that, can, stand, ham, an	Low-Front	64,65
ɔ	aw	paw, call, wrong, toss, fought	Low-Back	57,61,62
a	ah	rah, hot, star, bottom, rock	Low-Back	57,61,62

IPA PHONEMIC DIPHTHONGS (2-Vowel Glides):

aɪ	ah-ee	I, bye, lie, type, kind, rhyme	Low-Back, High-Front	56,61
aʊ	ah-oh	how, shout, round, towel, out	Low-Back, Mid-Back	56,61
ɔɪ	aw-ee	boy, hoist, broil, royal, toy	Low-Back, High-Front	61
ju	yo͞o	you, fuel, cute, regular, use	Blade-Pre-Pal., High-Back	16

BIBLIOGRAPHY

Adler, Sol. *"Bidialectalism? Mandatory or Elective?"* Washington D.C.: ASHA, 1987.

Berger, Mary I. Unpublished research for Thesis Statement: "American Black Dialects: Educational Decisions." Chicago, 1968.

Bountress, Nicholas G. *"The Ann Arbor Decision."* Washington D.C.: ASHA, 1979.

Burkland, Marjorie. Unpublished exercises and drills. Speech Dept., Evanston, IL: Evanston Township High School, 1983.

Chicago Public Schools. *Psycholinguistics Oral Language Program: A Bi-Dialectal Approach.* Chicago, 1968.

Chreist, Fred M. *Foreign Accent.* Englewood Cliffs, N.J.: Prentice Hall, 1987.

Cole, Lorraine. Lecture on "Black English." ASHA, 1980.

Dillard, J. L. *Black English.* New York: Random House, 1972.

Ehrlich, Eugene and Hand, Raymond Jr. *NBC Handbook of Pronunciation.* New York: Harper and Row, 1987.

Fisher, Hilda B. and Logemann, Jerilyn A. *The Fisher-Logemann Test of Articulation Competence.* Boston: Houghton Mifflin Co., 1971.

Labov, William. "Stages in the Acquisition of Standard English" from *Social Dialects and Language Learning.* Champaign: NCTE, 1964.

McCrum, Robert; Cran, William; MacNeil, Robert. *The Story of English.* New York: Viking, 1986.

McDavid, Raven I. "American Social Dialects." *College English* 26, No. 4. January, 1965.

Nilsen, Don L. F. and Nilsen, Alleen Pace. *Pronunciation Contrasts in English.* New York: Regents Publishing, 1973.

Pederson, Lee A. *"Some Structural Differences in the Speech of Chicago Negroes."* Social Dialects and Language Learning. Champaign: NCTE, 1964.

Smitherman, Geneva. *Talkin and Testifyin.* Boston: Houghton-Mifflin, 1977.

Stewart, William A. *"Urban Negro Speech: Sociolinguistic Factors Affecting English Teaching,"* Social Dialects and Language Learning. Champaign: NCTE, 1964.

Turner, Lorenzo D. *Africanisms in the Gullah Dialect.* Chicago: Univ. of Chicago Press, 1949.